A PRACTICUM EXERCISE
FOR
NITA

GENERAL/TRIAL FILE

EMPLOYMENT/LABOR LAW

Advocacy Training Options

- Trial (Court/Jury)
- Negotiation
- Mediation
- Motions / Oral Argument

Pat Rogers (Employee)

v.

Midstate University (Employer)

Pat Rogers (Employee)
v.
Midstate University (Employer)

By

John O. Sonsteng and Linda M. Thorstad

with Jennifer W. Miller

Address inquiries to:

Reprint Permission
National Institute for Trial Advocacy
1685 38th Street, Suite 200
Boulder, CO 80301
Phone: (800) 225-6482
Fax: (720) 890-7069
E-mail: permissions@nita.org

ISBN 978-1-60156-116-9
FBA1116

Printed in the United States of America

NITA PRACTICUM EXERCISE

The Nita Practicum Series is designed to be an effective tool for helping attorneys and students develop and improve effective **Advocacy Skills**.

The Practicum exercises are self contained and have all necessary information. No outside research is required.

NITA Advocacy Training Options

This Practicum exercise may be used in the following **Advocacy** Training Programs:

• Trial (Court/Jury) • Negotiation • Mediation • Motions/Oral Argument

This Practicum exercise contains the following:

- *Party and Witness Statements/Depositions*

  The statements/depositions of the parties and witnesses are included in the exercise materials.

- *Procedural and Factual History*

  The Procedural and Factual History provides an introduction to the facts of the exercise as well as the legal and factual background.

- *The Facts*

  The facts are complete.

- *Applicable Law*

  This section contains applicable law.

- *Case and Strategic Analysis*

  The case and strategic analysis is a preliminary guide. It provides the basis for a more sophisticated analysis, preparation, and performance.

Learning Materials

The Learning Materials are located at the end of this exercise.

- *Planning Guide and Checklist*

  The Planning Guide and Checklist is an outline that assists in the preparation of legal substance and presentation. It provides the basis for more detailed planning.

- *Learning Objectives*

  The Learning Objectives provide a method to measure achievement.

  > *Oral*—assists in planning and delivering the assigned oral skill.

  > *Written*—assists in developing and presenting both written and oral skills.

CONTENTS

Exhibits List [Exhibits located on CD]

    Exhibit 1: **Collective Bargaining Agreement—Article 28**
                  (Witnesses: Pat Rogers, Police Chief Troy, and President D. Laterno)

    Exhibit 2: **Metropolitan News [University Sells Soul for Alcohol Money]**
                  (Witnesses: Pat Rogers and President D. Laterno)

    Exhibit 3: **Metropolitan News [Opponents of Liquor Store Gift: Shame on 'U'!]**
                  (Witnesses: Pat Rogers, Police Chief Troy, and President D. Laterno)

    Exhibit 4: **Metropolitan News [Manager Wanted—Want Ad]**
                  (Witnesses: Pat Rogers, Police Chief Troy and President D. Laterno)

    Exhibit 5: **Rogers's Application Letter**
                  (Witnesses: Pat Rogers and President D. Laterno)

    Exhibit 6: **Rogers's Resume**
                  (Witnesses: Pat Rogers and President D. Laterno)

    Exhibit 7: **Letter of Hiring from Alex Margolis**
                  (Witnesses: Pat Rogers and President D. Laterno)

    Exhibit 8: **Rules of Employment and Management of the Off Campus Liquor Store**
                  (Witnesses: Pat Rogers, Police Chief Troy, and President D. Laterno)

ACKNOWLEDGMENTS

This NITA Practicum Exercise was successfully designed and tested at William Mitchell College of Law, St. Paul, Minnesota.

We gratefully acknowledge William Mitchell College of Law Legal Practicum and Advanced Advocacy students and adjunct faculty who critiqued this exercise and suggested improvements.

The following students from William Mitchell College of Law made major contributions to the NITA Practicum exercises: Sarah Bennett, Christine Eid, Lauralee Fritz, Mary Harens, Anne Howarth, Briana Isiminger, Jan Jeske, Kelly Martinez, Jessica Nault, Taylor Tarvestad, Jacob Thompson, Maureen Ventura, and Chong Ye.

Special thanks to our families who stood beside us through the NITA Practicum Exercise development, creation, editing, re-editing, proofing, and re-proofing for days, weeks, months, and, in some instances, years. They deserve credit for their involvement, suggestions, patience, inspiration and encouragement.

Diane, Michael, David, and Molly Sonsteng

John, Troy, and Millie Thorstad

Jonny, Jake, and Jada Miller

VERY IMPORTANT

DIRECTIONS FOR DETERMINING DATES, AGES, AND APPLICABLE LAW

In order to keep this exercise current and workable for any time and place, *dates, ages, and statutes* **must** *be inserted where indicated by a blank line and a bold instruction in parentheses.*

Dates

Use a current calendar. Dates are to be calculated from the date assigned by the instructor. Should an event occur on a holiday, the holiday should be ignored unless specifically indicated by the exercise or the instructor.

Dates are *not* an issue in an exercise unless specifically indicated by the instructor.

The following formula will permit correct dates to be inserted where necessary.

* All dates following the assignment of the exercise are indicated by a "plus" (+) sign, followed by the number of days, weeks, months, or years to be counted:

> (day +1), (week +1), (month +1), (year +1)

* All dates preceding the assignment of the exercise are indicated by a "minus" (-) sign, followed by the number of days, weeks, months, or years to be counted:

> (day -1), (week -1), (month -1), (year -1)

* The date assigned by the instructor is:

> (day 0), (week 0), (month 0), and (year 0).

* **NEVER** count the current day, week, or month when calculating the dates.

How to Calculate and Insert the Dates

Example 1:

* The exercise is assigned on **Friday, July 29, 2011.**

    * **Before** the date is inserted, the exercise reads as follows:

*We purchased the stock on __ (***Wednesday, Week -3).***

* Do not count the current week. Count back three weeks. The date that must be inserted is July 6, 2011.

    * **After** inserting this date, the exercise will now read:

We purchased the stock on *July 6, 2011* **(Wednesday, Week -3).**

Example 2:

* The exercise is assigned on **Monday, August 8, 2011.**

    * ***Before*** the date is inserted, the exercise reads as follows:

I bought the house on _____ **(1st Wednesday, Month -28).**

* Do not count the current month. Count back twenty-eight months. The date that must be inserted is Wednesday, April 2, 2009.

    * ***After*** inserting this date, the exercise will now read:

I bought the house on <u>*Wednesday, April 2, 2009*</u>. **(1st Wednesday, Month -28).**

Ages

The ages of clients and other people may be found throughout the exercise.

Example:

* I was born on April 18, _____**(Year -48).**

This indicates that the person would be forty-eight years old.

Applicable Law

Unless otherwise indicated by the exercise, the law of your jurisdiction will apply.

Example:

* ***Before*** the current statutory reference is inserted, the exercise reads as follows:

The above-named juvenile is alleged to be delinquent pursuant to _____ **(state statute)** because the juvenile has violated a state/local law as follows . . . .

* ***After*** inserting the current statutory reference, the exercise will now read:

The above-named juvenile is alleged to be delinquent pursuant to <u>*Nita Stat. 609.015*</u> **(state statute)** because the juvenile has violated a state/local law as follows . . . .

PROCEDURAL AND FACTUAL HISTORY

Assume the days and dates in the exercise are accurate.

The following facts and procedures are agreed to by the parties and must be accepted by them. These facts may be considered as agreed-upon evidence and may be used in the opening statement and closing argument.

Introduction

This dispute centers around the discharge of an employee, Pat Rogers, by Midstate University. Pat Rogers is a member of the State Professional Employee Union (SPEU). Under the terms of the Collective Bargaining Agreement between Midstate University and State Professional Employee Union (SPEU), the University installed the Rules of Employment and Management of the Off Campus Liquor Store, which governed the employment of Pat Rogers. The University alleges Pat Rogers violated Rule 6 of Employment and Management of the Off Campus Liquor Store by knowingly selling alcohol to an intoxicated person and terminated Rogers. The employee's union (SPEU) filed a grievance on behalf of the employee.

Under the terms of the Collective Bargaining Agreement, Rogers has elected to have the matter heard at trial by a judge or jury.

Midstate University has been under considerable financial pressure for the last five years. The legislature has continually reduced funding, and many programs have been cut. The president of the University has worked very hard to create new sources of funding.

One year ago, Martin and Julia Wong made a substantial contribution to Midstate University. The Wongs were both graduates of the University and felt the University gave them an opportunity for an education and their subsequent success. The Wongs owned a liquor store located across the street from Midstate University campus. They donated the liquor store and its proceeds to the University. The Off Campus Liquor store has an annual net return of at least $1,000,000. The Wongs placed conditions on their contribution:

- The liquor store could not be sold, and

- The annual proceeds had to be spent for developing or continuing programs that assist minority persons to compete successfully for admission to the University and to successfully complete a university education.

The importance of this gift cannot be understated, as all affirmative action programs have been terminated by the state and there are no other funds for a program of this nature.

The gift was controversial. Over the last five years the use of alcohol by students on campuses throughout the state, at both public and private schools, has reached serious levels. There were three student deaths in the last year attributed to alcohol. Student binge drinking has become a serious problem, and Midstate University has passed strict rules about the use of alcohol on campus and by underage persons. The newspaper as well as some legislators have been critical of the University's acceptance of the gift and the conditions. One headline read: "University Sells Soul for Alcohol Money."

The president of the University understands the problem, but concludes the money is critical for necessary programs. The president believes strict management rules can prevent abuse or problems.

Working with the University attorney, the president developed rules for the liquor store.

About eight months ago, after the gift was accepted and the University had taken possession of the liquor store, Midstate University advertised for a manager for the store. Pat Rogers, a single parent of two young children, answered the ad. Rogers was the successful owner of a small chain of bagel/coffee shops near campus and in some of the trendy shopping areas. Although successful in the bagel business, Rogers wanted a more stable life, wanted to be able to have more time with the children, and found the benefits of the University system very attractive. Midstate University provides reduced tuition for children of employees at the University-run elementary school and high school. The University also has excellent health and retirement benefits.

Although Rogers had no experience with managing a liquor store, Rogers is a very good business person and was the best candidate for the job. Rogers sold the bagel/coffee businesses and began employment eleven months ago.

On the day that is the basis for this matter, Pat Rogers was working alone in the liquor store at approximately 8:00 p.m. Rogers acknowledges selling a bottle of liquor to Professor Erik Tolefson, a retired Midstate University Professor of Norwegian studies and philosophy. Rogers said Tolefson did not appear intoxicated. Midstate University Police Chief, M. J. Troy, watched Tolefson when he entered the liquor store and thought Tolefson was drunk.

After Tolefson left the store, Troy administered three field sobriety tests to Tolefson.[1] Troy asked him to perform: 1) the walk-and-turn test—Tolefson staggered and nearly fell on turning; 2) the one-leg stand—Tolefson could not stand on one leg; and 3) Horizontal Gaze Nystagmus (HGN)—Troy held an index finger about a foot in front of Tolefson's eyes and asked Tolefson to follow Troy's finger with his eyes as Troy's finger moved right to left and back slowly. Tolefson could not follow Troy's finger with

---

[1]**Field Sobriety.** The three field sobriety tests that comprise the Standardized Field Sobriety Test (SFST) battery are: 1) the walk-and-turn test, 2) the one-leg stand test, 3) the Horizontal Gaze Nystagmus test. The Horizontal Gaze Nystagmus (HGN) is used as an indicator of intoxication as the eye movements of a sober person differ greatly from those of an impaired person. Nystagmus is a naturally occurring phenomenon of the eyes; drugs and/or alcohol increase or exaggerate the twitching or jerking of the eyes.

Once the officer determines that the suspect does not have a medical condition that would affect the eyes, the officer conducts the HGN test. A penlight or even a finger is tracked in front of the suspect's eyes—about one foot distant—and the suspect is asked to follow the light or finder with the eyes.

The examiner is looking for three indicators of impairment in each eye: if the eye cannot follow a moving object smoothly; if jerking is distinct when the eye is at maximum deviation; and if the angle of onset of jerking of the eyeball, instead of smoothly tracking, is within forty-five degrees of center. If, between the two eyes, four or more clues appear, the suspect likely has a BAC of .10 or greater. http://www.horizontalgazenystagmus.com/horizontalgazenystagmustests.htmal and http://www.nhtsa.gov/people/injury/enforce/nystagmus/hgntxt.html.

his eyes. Tolefson failed the sobriety tests. Troy also administrated a Preliminary Breath Test (PBT)[2] breath test to Tolefson and learned he had a .12 percent blood alcohol level.

After reviewing Troy's report, the president of Midstate University fired Rogers. The parties have agreed that the issue is whether the employee was discharged for just cause. The Union has filed a grievance in this matter on behalf of Pat Rogers. The Union has requested an expedited arbitration hearing pursuant to Article 28 of the Collective Bargaining Agreement. The terms of the Collective Bargaining Agreement permit the employee to bypass arbitration and elect to have a trial before a judge or jury. Pat Rogers has chosen to bypass arbitration and have a trial.

Issues Raised

(These issues do not limit participants. Other appropriate issues may be raised.)

- A. Whether the employee was discharged for just cause
- B. Just cause for discipline
- C. Just cause for extent of discipline
- D. Progressive discipline
- E. Remedies in Arbitration
    - —Termination
    - —Suspension
    - —Reinstatement with or without back pay
- F. Remedies in Trial
    - —Damages

---

[2]**Preliminary Breath Test (PBT) Reliability.** In general, chemical tests such as breath analysis are considered reliable scientific methods of determining intoxication, and the results of such tests are generally admissible to prove intoxication. However, the results of preliminary breath tests (PBT) are not admissible for that purpose, but only to show the existence of probable cause for arrest. The test is given at the scene of a traffic stop to determine whether the blood alcohol concentration is sufficient to support an arrest. A chemical test to determine intoxication has been said to be considered a reliable scientific method, the validity of which is not open to serious objection.

Preliminary breath tests are inadmissible and cannot be used as evidence to prove someone is intoxicated. The results may be used to determine whether more accurate testing is appropriate and thus be admissible for the limited purpose of showing probable cause for arrest.

A preliminary breath test may be given as a field sobriety test upon a police officer's "reasonable artculable suspicion" that a person has violated a statute prohibiting driving while impaired. The officer must have "reason to believe" from a person's manner of driving that the driver may be violating the impaired driving laws.

The officer's reasonable suspicion may include their subjective opinion based on observation and perception, including the odor of alcohol, slurred speech, loss of balance or dexterity, or any number of observable factors such as improper driving, a tip from a reliable source, or the admission of alcohol consumption.

Preliminary breath screening test results are admissible in prosecutions as evidence in a civil proceeding. Although the evidence is supposedly admissible on a motion to suppress in a criminal case, it may not be used in te criminal trial itself. Giving a preliminary breath test does not foreclose other tests under the implied consent law.

      • Economic

      • Physical

      • Mental

  G. Reasonableness of the procedure for termination and the application to this employee

  H. Sufficiency of the notice of the rule

  I. Past practices

Witnesses

(The witnesses may be male or female)

Unless otherwise advised, the parties may not call any of the other parties' witnesses in their case-in-chief.

Employer

    M. J. Troy, *Police Chief*

    D. Laterno, *Midstate University President*

Employee and Union

    Pat Rogers

Employer

Midstate University

    Midstate University was founded in 1900 as an agricultural and liberal arts institution and is located in Silver Springs, the second largest city in Nita. The University's location enhances the traditional classroom experience by providing students greater opportunities in resources, contacts with business and government leaders, employment, and internships.

    With an enrollment of more than 22,000, Midstate University prides itself on specialized attention to each student. Although the University's students come from almost every state in the United States and 120 foreign countries, 55 percent are from Nita and represent nearly all counties in the state. Midstate University offers BA, BS, MA, MS, and PhD degrees in seventy-five courses of study. Midstate College of Law, an affiliate of Midstate University, offers both an LLM and a JD degree.

    The 200-acre campus is modern and accessible and at the same time retains the flavor of the University's 100-plus year heritage. More than fifty pieces of sculpture by internationally known artists adorn the campus. During the past twenty years, Midstate University has more than doubled its instructional space, adding major buildings for art, engineering, health sciences, biological sciences, physical education, music, dance, and liberal arts and sciences. Approximately 120 social and special interest clubs provide opportunities for students to meet and work with others who share their interests. Ten national sororities and ten national fraternities are active on campus. Midstate University is a Division I institution and has teams in tennis, cross-country, basketball, track, football, soccer, golf, bowling, crew rowing, men's baseball, and women's volleyball and softball. The men's and women's bowling teams have won numerous national championships. The University's mascot name, the "Schooners," reflects the national heritage of the heartland—the Prairie Schooners (covered wagons) that brought settlers across the country to settle the nation.

MSU has 479 full-time faculty and forty-one part-time faculty. Of the total, 73 percent have earned the highest degree in their field. Of all undergraduate credit hours, 62 percent are taught by full-time faculty. The average age of the faculty is fifty-four; 56 percent of the faculty are males and 44 percent are females.

Police Chief M. J. Troy

Age:	Thirty-five.
Married:	Married, three children.
Education:	BS in Police Administration, Midstate University, _____ **(Year -13)**.
	Postgraduate work in business administration, Portland University, _____ **(Year -11)**.

Employment:

- Police Officer, Portland, Oregon, _____ **(Year -13) to** _____ **(Year -11)**.

- Police Officer, Midstate University, _____ **(Year -10) to** _____ **(Year -6)**.

- Midstate University Chief of Police, _____ **(Year -6) to** _____ **present**.

Additional achievements:

- Teaches courses and seminars at Midstate University and to the Nita Bar Association on alcohol policies and their enforcement.

- Articles published: "Spotting the Drunk Driver" and "Drinking Yourself to Death," both published in the *National Police Officers Magazine*, _____(Year -2).

D. Laterno

Age:	Fifty-three, born Dec. 23, _____(Year -53).
Married:	Married, no children.
Education:	BA, Economics, Louisiana State University, _____(Year -21).
	MBA, Harvard University, _____(Year -19).
	PhD, Business Administration, Harvard University, _____(Year -16).

Employment:

- Associate Professor of Marketing, Midstate University, _____(Year -16) to _____(Year -10).

- Professor of Marketing and Finance, Midstate University, _____(Year -10) to _____(Year -8).

- Acting Dean, College of Business, Midstate University, _____(Year -8) to _____(Year -6).

- Dean of Business College, Ball State University, _____(Year -6) to _____(Year -3).

- President, Midstate University, _____(Year -3) to _____ present.

Publications:

Thesis: *Business and Education—An Educational Conundrum*, _____(Year -16).

Alcohol and Money: A Dangerous Mix on University Campuses, _____(Year -5).

"Managing a Stressed University," *National Education Forum*, _____(Year -2).

Alex Margolis

(Not available as a witness)

Age:	Thirty-two, born July 15, _____(Year -32).
Married:	Married, two children.
Education:	BS Business and Accounting / Human Resources, Midstate University, _____(Year -10).
	MBA, Human Resource Management, Lincoln University, _____(Year -4).

Employment:

- Associate Director of Human Resources, Lincoln University, _____(Year -10) to _____(Year -7).

- Assistant Director of Human Resources, Lincoln University, _____(Year -7) to _____(Year -2).

- Director of Human Resources, Midstate University, _____(Year -2) to present.

John Marden

(Not available as a witness)

Age:	Twenty-six, born Jan. 2, _____**(Year -26)**.
Married:	Single.
Education:	BA, English, West Hills University, _____**(Year -4)**.
Employment:	

- Midstate University, Assistant to the President, _____**(Year -2)** to _____**(Fri., Week -3)**.

Professor Erik Tolefson

(Not available as a witness)

Age:	Seventy-one, born March 2, _____**(Year -71)**.
Married:	Married (Ingrid), five children, eleven grandchildren, thirteen great-grandchildren.
Education:	Doctorate Degree in Norwegian Studies and Philosophy from the University of Oslo, Oslo, Norway, _____**(Year -43)**.

Employment:

- Professor of Norwegian Studies and Philosophy at Midstate University from _____**(Year -40)** to ___**(Year -2)** (now retired).
- Volunteer Greeter/Dosa at the Sons of Norway Museum.
- Volunteer Gardener at the Horticulture Society's Peace Gardens.
- Volunteer Norwegian Language Instructor for Elementary Students.

Publications:

> *Norwegian Songs and Poetry from the Fjords*
>
> *Clashing Scandinavian Philosophies*
>
> *Theoretical Studies on the Native Sami Culture of Norway*
>
> *Botanical Guide to Torsdala and the Lillehammar Region*

Employee and Union

State Professional Employee Union (SPEU)

In _____ **(Year -5)**, a budgetary crisis in the state brought new concerns to the state professional employees relating to job security and decline of service to clients. A newly formed State Professional Employee Union (SPEU) broke away from the American Association of State, County, and Municipal Employees (AASCME) and the Midstate University Union of Teachers and Employees (MUUTE). Both organizations previously represented professional employees working for state agencies, schools, and universities directed and funded by the State of Nita.

The Union (SPEU) represents 950 Midstate University employees.

Pat Rogers

Age:	Thirty-five, born October 31, _____(Year -35).
Married:	Spouse (deceased). Twin daughters, Sheri Lynn and Mary Rose, age six years old.
Education:	BA, History, University of Wisconsin, _____(Year -13).
	MBA, Business Management, Midstate University, _____(Year -11).

Employment:

- Clerk, White Wolf Coffee Shops, Inc., _____(Year -13) to _____ (Year -12).
- Asst. Store Manager, White Wolf Coffee Shops, Inc., _____(Year -12) to _____(Year -11).
- Store Manager, White Wolf Coffee Shops, Inc., _____(Year -11) to _____(Year -9).
- Owner/Operator/Manager, The Coffee Shop and Bakery, (single shop), _____(Year -9) to _____(Year -7).
- Owner/Operator/Manager, The Coffee Shop and Bakery, (four coffee shops),

  _____(Year -7) to _____(Year -1).
- Off Campus Liquor Store, _____(First Monday, Month -9) to ____(Month -5).

Party and Witness Depositions and/or Statements

The letters, statements, and reports are comprised of information provided by witnesses and have been adopted by them as true and correct. Accordingly, they may be used as is appropriate under the agreed-upon rules of evidence. When testifying, each witness may only add nonsubstantial facts that are consistent with the case file. Significant substantive facts may not be added.

Exhibits and Documents

The exhibits and documents are all authentic. Witness testimony provides both legal and persuasive foundation for exhibits. The exhibits may be marked separately (i.e., Exhibit 1, Exhibit 2, etc.). If the exhibit has more than one page, the first page of the exhibit can serve as the exhibit number, and the number of pages contained in the exhibit can be found at the top of the page.

All exhibits should be offered for admission and be received into evidence before the exhibit can be used. The agreed-upon rules of evidence apply in regard to admission of exhibits.

THE FACTS

DETAILED TIMELINE OF SIGNIFICANT DATES

Month -12
- First Monday   Wongs give Off Campus Liquor Store to Midstate University.

Month -11
- First Monday   Off Campus Liquor Store ad for manager runs.
- Second Monday   Pat Rogers applies for Off Campus Liquor Store manager's job.
- Last Thursday   Hiring letter from Alex Margolis.

Month -9
- First Monday   Rogers begins employment at Midstate University's Off Campus Liquor Store.

Month -3
- First Monday   Rogers's six-month job review.

Week -6
- Friday   Rogers sells liquor to Tolefson.
- Friday   Initial Report of M. J. Troy regarding Tolefson.

Week -5
- Monday   Letter from Rogers to Laterno hoping not to be fired.
- Wednesday   Letter from Laterno to Rogers firing Rogers.
- Friday   Metropolitan News article regarding Rogers.

Week -4
- Monday   State Public Employee's Union (SPEU) files Grievance on behalf of Pat Rogers.
- Tuesday   Letter from Rogers to Laterno—angry about being fired. Rogers elects to bypass arbitration and have matter heard by judge/jury trial.
- Friday   Letter from Laterno to Rogers refuting statements in news article.

Week -3
- Monday   Letter from Rogers to Laterno (Rogers electing a trial).
- Monday   Rogers files Compliant (Rogers chooses to bypass arbitration and have matter decided at trial).
- Wednesday   Midstate University files Answer.

Day -10
- Follow-Up Police Report from M. J. Troy.

Day -9
- Letter from Pat Rogers to Union advocate explaining what happened.

Day -8
- Letter from Laterno to law firm representing Midstate University explaining what happened.

January 15, _____ **(Year -5)**

TO: All Midstate University Employees

FROM: Lester Evansvold, Midstate University President and
            Francis Jilek, State Professional Employee Union (SPEU) President

We are pleased to announce after taking the vote, the State Professional Employee Union (SPEU) now represents all nonfaculty employees of Midstate University. Midstate University and SPEU have ratified the Collective Bargaining Agreement effective as of this date. The Collective Bargaining Agreement is attached.

Attachment: Collective Bargaining Agreement

COLLECTIVE BARGAINING AGREEMENT

(Page 1 of 2)

Article 28—Collective Bargaining Agreement between
Midstate University and State Professional Employee Union (SPEU)
Adopted January 15, _____ (Year -5)
[The Agreement has been edited for this exercise.]

A. Nothing in this Agreement is intended to circumscribe or modify the existing right of Midstate University to:

(1) direct the work of its employees.

(2) hire, promote, assign, transfer, and retain as to position with the Company.

(3) demote, suspend, reduce in pay, or discharge employees for just cause.

(4) maintain the efficiency of company operations.

(5) take actions as may be necessary to carry out the mission and vision of the Company.

(6) determine the methods, means, and personnel by which operations are to be carried on.

(7) develop and implement reasonable* rules of employment including schedules and time keeping.

(8) promulgate reasonable* reporting and record keeping obligations and procedures in policies adopted under the Collective Bargaining Agreement.

*Reasonable: being in accordance with reason; not extreme or excessive; moderate and fair, and possessing sound judgment.

B. Disciplinary actions may, at the employer's discretion, include warnings, suspensions, and discharges. Any employee disciplined or discharged shall be entitled to file a grievance through the Employee's Union within thirty (30) days of written notification of discipline. The grievance must set out the basis for the grievance. If requested in writing by the Union, an expedited hearing will be held with the Union within thirty (30) days of the Disciplinary Action or Discharge Violation.

1. **Violation of critical work rules.** Critical work rules are defined as rules that endanger health or safety. A violation of a critical work rule may subject the Employee to immediate termination.

2. **Violation of noncritical work rules.** Noncritical work rules are defined as rules that do not endanger health or safety.

Steps to Discipline:

Step 1: A first violation. When an Employee violates a noncritical work rule, the Employee shall receive an oral notice. Verification of this oral notice shall be placed in writing in the Employee's personnel file.

Step 2: A second violation. Employee shall receive a written reprimand to be placed in the Employee's file. The Employee shall meet with the Human Resources Director.

Step 3: A third violation subjects the Employee to a written reprimand and a suspension without pay for up to thirty (30) days. The Employee and the Union Steward may meet with the Human Resources Director prior to the enforcement of the suspension.

Step 4: A fourth violation of a noncritical work rule will subject the Employee to the immediate termination of employment. The basis for the discipline, including termination, must be set out in writing and must state all grounds for the discipline. The written notice of discipline must be provided to the Employee and the State Professional Employee Union (SPEU) representing the Employee.

COLLECTIVE BARGAINING AGREEMENT

(Page 2 of 2)

C. The Parties to the Collective Bargaining Agreement may agree that this matter may be resolved through negotiation or mediation. Absent such an agreement, the matter will be resolved through arbitration. However, when an Employee is terminated the Employee may elect to have the matter heard by a judge or jury. (See E. below.)

D. **Arbitration**

- *Burden of Proof*: The Employer shall have the burden of proof by a preponderance of the evidence that there was just cause for discipline of the Employee and just cause for the degree of discipline.
- Disciplinary arbitrators shall render determinations of a violation of work rules and the appropriateness of proposed penalties, and shall have the authority to resolve a claimed failure to follow the procedural provisions of this Agreement. Disciplinary arbitrators shall neither add to, subtract from, nor modify the provisions of this Agreement. In an arbitration, the Employee may be terminated, suspended, or reinstated with or without back pay. Additional damages are not available in an arbitration.
- The Employee (grievant) shall be represented by the Union.
- The Employer shall present the first opening statement and the concluding final argument.
- The Employee (grievant) shall not have a rebuttal final argument.
- The arbitrator shall determine the Rules of Evidence that shall apply.

E. **Trial to Judge or Jury**

- If an Employee is terminated, the Employee may elect to have the matter heard by a judge or jury.
- The Employee must notify the Employer in writing of this election within thirty (30) days of the Employee's termination. If the thirtieth (30th) day falls on a Saturday; Sunday; or legal, national, or state holiday, the thirtieth (30th) day shall be the next full work day.
- Upon election to try the matter to a judge or jury, the Employee must file a complaint in state court within thirty (30) days of this election.
- The Employer must file an answer within thirty (30) days of receiving notice of the complaint.
- The Union shall not be required to represent the Employee in a trial. (The Union may choose to represent the Employee.)
- *Burden of Proof*: The Employee shall have the burden of proof by a preponderance of the evidence that there was insufficient cause for termination.
- In a trial to a judge or jury, the Employee may seek damages in addition to the remedies provided by the Collective Bargaining Agreement. The Employee has the burden of proving damages by a preponderance of the evidence.
- The Employee shall be the plaintiff, and the Employer shall be the defendant.
- The Employee shall present the first opening statement and the concluding final argument.
- The Employer shall not have a rebuttal final argument.
- The Employee must present evidence first.
- The Rules of Evidence, Procedure, and Law of the jurisdiction where the complaint is filed shall govern but shall not amend any terms of this agreement.

F. **Discovery Depositions**

- The Employer and the Employee may take discovery depositions of witnesses or parties.
- The depositions are limited to three per side.
- A deposition of a witness or a party may not exceed thirty (30) minutes.
- Upon written application and with good cause shown, the thirty (30) minute time limit for taking a deposition and the number of persons to be deposed may be increased.

METROPOLITAN NEWS

L. Marie, Publisher—John Oliver, Editor

In the News:

Weekend "Knit-A-Thon" at the Springs Mall Produces 933½ Pairs of Socks for Homeless and Soldiers

Silver Springs Attorney Accidentally Sues Himself on Land Deal

_____ **(First Monday, Month -12)**

University Sells Soul for Alcohol Money

Midstate University President, D. Laterno, announced today that Midstate University graduates Martin and Julia Wong made a substantial gift to the University—the Off Campus Liquor Store. The Wongs, who have been successful in a number of business enterprises, told *Metropolitan News* they wanted to give back to the University and that they were concerned the Legislature had cut programs for minority students. The Wongs said they could not have attended college without programs similar to ones recently cut by the legislature. Laterno, announcing the Wongs' gift, which would likely give the University at least $1 million annually, said the University welcomed the gift and believed it would provide important benefits to the University and its students. The Wongs and Laterno said they were shocked to learn of negative reactions from students, faculty, and parents to the Wongs' gift.

Laterno acknowledged some recent problems with alcohol on campus and was aware that the managers of Wongs' liquor store had not been responsible. Laterno said that with strict rules and consistent enforcement, the University expected few, if any, problems in the future.

John and Anna Becklund, parents of James Becklund, a first-year student who died of an overdose of alcohol at a fraternity party last year, said they were stunned that the University accepted "liquor money." Mrs. Becklund said that the University should never accept liquor money, even if the programs it would support "were the most wonderful in the world." She called the Wongs' gift "the Devil's money." Mr. Becklund agreed with his wife and said, "The University has sold its soul for alcohol money."

The Wongs said they were confident the details of the gift could be worked out and that the University would be able to accept their gift with their restrictions. Those restrictions prohibit the University from selling the liquor store once it has been accepted and require that all net profits from its operation, in recent years more than $1 million annually, be used to develop or continue outreach programs assisting minority persons to compete for University admission and to complete their education. One unnamed source told *Metropolitan News* there would be continuing protests if the University accepts the gift.

METROPOLITAN NEWS

L. Marie, Publisher—John Oliver, Editor

In the News:

> **Newly Camouflage-Painted Army Reserve Truck Disappears—Search Underway in Cold Creek Forest**
>
> **Red Tape Holds Up New Bridge Spanning Springs Creek**

_____ **(Second Monday, Month -12)**

Opponents of Liquor Store Gift: Shame on 'U'!

"Midstate University sold out for the almighty dollar," said Sarah Lincoln and James Oliver, co-chairpersons of Students Against Drugs and Alcohol (SADA), a student organization formed to prevent alcohol and drugs on campus and to promote responsible behavior among students. In a desperate attempt to make up for cuts in appropriations by the legislature, the University accepted a liquor store located just off campus as a gift. The store was given to the University by a wealthy alumni couple for the purpose of supplying money for minority affairs programs that were cut by lack of legislative funding. "While this may sound like a good idea at first glance, it is just a desperate attempt to salvage programs cut by the legislature," Lincoln said.

The University has recently experienced serious problems with drinking on campus, drinking by underage persons, and binge drinking. In the last three years, three students died from alcohol-related problems, two in car accidents and one from an overdose of alcohol at a fraternity party on campus. "Sometimes we have to stop and think. What kind of message are we sending to our children?" asked the mayor of the city, Andrew Peters. University President Laterno responded, "We understand how some may think we are giving the wrong message. However, the University has instituted strict policies against drinking. As we all know, drinking itself is not illegal. Abuse of alcohol is the problem. We can never stop the drinking, but we can teach our students to be responsible."

"The gift of Mr. and Mrs. Wong came at a time when money problems forced the legislature to cut significant programs," Laterno said, "and income from the liquor store will permit the University to reestablish programs that will assist the University, its students, and our community."

Laterno continued, "We will establish strict rules for the liquor store to assure there will be no violation of any laws or University policies."

A coalition of campus organizations, churches, and political organizations plans to protest the University's action in accepting the Wongs' gift. Marlys Massterson, a spokesperson for the coalition said, "There has to be another way to keep these programs. Good programs should never be funded by booze money."

METROPOLITAN NEWS

L. Marie, Publisher—John Oliver, Editor

_____ **(First Monday, Month -11)**

Advertising Section

Want Ad

Manager Wanted

Midstate University seeks experienced, responsible retail business manager to direct its liquor store operation. This University-owned business was donated to the University on the condition that all proceeds be used for minority affairs programs. The University, committed to its zero-tolerance campus alcohol policy and to enforcement of restrictions on the sale and misuse of alcohol, seeks person of demonstrated responsibility to operate this business. Starting salary is in the mid-50s, with potential for bonuses and salary growth. Attractive health care and retirements plans included. As a manager in the University system, employee will receive a three-quarters tuition waiver in the University educational system (including our K–12 school) for children of employee.

Applications should be directed to:

Department of Personnel

Midstate University

10500 Campus Drive

Silver Springs, Nita

Midstate University is an equal opportunity employer.

Pat Rogers
7044 Balsam Trail
Silver Springs, Nita 55515
999-869-9053

_____ (Second Monday, Month -11)

Midstate University
Department of Personnel
10500 Campus Drive
Silver Springs, Nita

Dear Administrator,

Please accept my application for the position of manager of the liquor store operation owned by the University. I am well aware of the controversy surrounding the gift of the liquor store to the University. I, too, am concerned about the abuse of alcohol by young people and the problems that abuse has led to on our University campuses. However, this gift provides resources that are vital to the growth of our University, offering more opportunities to those who may not otherwise be able to obtain a University education. With careful management and close attention to standards and rules, I believe the liquor store operation can be run appropriately and will not become a liability for the University or its students.

I have extensive experience in management and in working with young people, who are often employed in the coffee house business. My experience will serve the University well if I am hired as the manager of the liquor store operation. I look forward to the opportunity to interview for this position.

Sincerely,

Pat Rogers

Pat Rogers

_____ **(Second Monday, Month -11)**

Pat Rogers
7044 Balsam Trail
Silver Springs, Nita 55515
999-869-9053

Education   Bachelor's Degree in History, University of Wisconsin, _____(Year -13).

MBA Business Management, Midstate University, _____(Year -3).

Job History   Employee of White Wolf Coffee Shops, Inc., ____(Year -13) to ____(Year -12).

Assistant Store Manager, White Wolf Coffee Shops, Inc., _____(Year -12) to _____(Year -11).

Store Manager, White Wolf Coffee Shops, Inc., ____(Year -11) to ____(Year -9).

Owner/Operator/Manager of The Coffee Shop and Bakery, Inc., (single shop), _____(Year -9) to _____(Year -7).

Owner/Operator/Manager of The Coffee Shop and Bakery, Inc., (four coffee shops), _____(Year -7) through _____(Year -1).

**Management
Experience**   Eighty employees—The Coffee Shop and Bakery, Inc., includes part-time and full-time store employees, two-person secretarial staff, six assistant managers, and business manager.

**Volunteer and
Community Activities**

- Member and Vice-President for Chamber of Commerce. As a member of the Chamber of Commerce, I donate all leftover baked goods from my bakery at end of each business day to homeless shelters.
- Member of Habitat for Humanity.
- Member of Greenpeace.
- Volunteer reader at Northcrest Elementary School.

Midstate University

10500 Campus Drive

Silver Springs, Nita 55515

_____ **(Last Thursday, Month -11)**

Pat Rogers
7044 Balsam Trail
Silver Springs, Nita 55515

Dear Pat Rogers,

Following up on my phone call to you yesterday, I am pleased you will accept our job offer. It was a pleasure to meet with you two weeks ago. As you know, we heard from many qualified applicants for the position as manager of the University's liquor store operation. We are delighted to offer you the position. You were, by far, the best candidate for the job. Your experience and sensitivity to the issues will serve the University and its students very well. University President, D. Laterno, has been informed of our decision and is happy you have decided to come onboard at the University.

As I stated to you, your starting salary will be $55,000. You will have opportunities for increases and promotions within the University management system.

In response to some of the questions you asked me yesterday, you and your family will receive full health and dental coverage on the day you start with us. Your retirement will vest at the end of your six-month probationary period. As soon as you come to work, your two children will be able to enroll tuition-free in the University laboratory-elementary school, and should you remain employed with the University, your children will receive 3/4 tuition waivers through high school. If your children qualify academically for attendance at the University, they will receive 3/4 tuition waivers for the four-year undergraduate program at the University.

I understand that it will take a month for you to wind down your business operations, therefore we will look forward to you starting on the job on _____ **(First Monday, Month -9)**.

I have enclosed the special Rules of Employment and Management of the Off Campus Liquor Store. These Rules were adopted under the provisions of the Article 28 of the Collective Bargaining Agreement between Midstate University and the State Professional Employee Union (SPEU). They were approved by me and the Union Steward, Margaret Harmon.

Sincerely,

Alex Margolis

Alex Margolis
Director of Personnel
Midstate University

RULES OF EMPLOYMENT AND MANAGEMENT OF
THE OFF CAMPUS LIQUOR STORE

Developed in accordance with the Collective Bargaining Agreement, Article 28 between

Midstate University and State Professional Employee Union (SPEU)

Adopted _____(Month -11)

[The Rules have been edited for this Exercise.]

Rule 6: Sale of Alcohol to Minors or Intoxicated Persons

- No alcohol will be sold to an underage person.

- Employees are required to obtain identification of anyone who is not clearly of a legal age.

- No alcohol can knowingly be sold to a person who is intoxicated.

    - Intoxicated is defined to mean anyone over .08% blood alcohol.

    - Knowingly is defined as: knowing or should have known the buyer was intoxicated.

- A violation of any provision of Rule 6 is a violation of a Critical Work Rule under Article 28, B(1) of the Collective Bargaining Agreement (CBA), and the employee is subject to immediate termination.

- An employee terminated under the provision of Rule 6 and Article 28 of the Collective Bargaining Agreement (CBA) will lose all University benefits except for accrued and vested retirement funds.

Approved under Article 28 of the Collective Bargaining Agreement between Midstate University and the State Professional Employee Union (SPEU) that was adopted, _____(Year -5).

Alex Margolis

Alex Margolis
Director of Personnel, Midstate University

Margaret Harmon

Margaret Harmon
Union Steward SPEU, Local #1234

MIDSTATE UNIVERSITY

SIX-MONTH PROBATIONARY PERIOD JOB REVIEW

_____ **(First Monday, Month -3)**

Subject:	Pat Rogers
Position:	Manager of the Off Campus Liquor Store
Starting Date:	_____ **(First Monday, Month -9)**
Evaluator:	Alex Margolis
Recommendation:	Retention as employee

I have spoken to Pat Rogers, interviewed employees, looked at the management and financial records of the Off Campus Liquor Store, and determined the following: Pat Rogers is an excellent financial manager. Rogers has exceeded all financial projections for the operation. Rogers is a good personnel manager. Some of the employees who worked at the store before Rogers took over as manager were concerned with the strict rules that were imposed. The employees were not specific. I believe that some of their concern was due to a change in management style. However, this is something we may have to address later. Of more concern is Rogers's work with other managers within the system. Rogers seems to be somewhat of a loner and may not be perceived as a team player. Rogers showed impatience at the biweekly management team meetings and the monthly one-on-one meetings with supervisors. Rogers said on a number of occasions that the meetings got in the way of work on the job. Rogers has to understand the importance of teamwork and how various insights of all management personnel can improve the University system as a whole. Part of the problem may be the independence Rogers experienced as a small business owner and the difficulty Rogers has assimilating into the larger bureaucracy of the University.

Nevertheless, I highly recommend retention. Rogers is a valuable addition to our management team.

MIDSTATE UNIVERSITY POLICE DEPARTMENT

Incident Report

_____ **(Friday, Week -6)**

TO: File

FROM: Midstate University Chief of Police, M. J. Troy

RE: Pat Rogers

Following a conversation yesterday with University President, D. Laterno, I scheduled myself to conduct a stakeout of the Off Campus Liquor store located just off campus on 9191 Campus Drive. As we discussed, there have been a number of rumors concerning the sale of liquor to underage people at the liquor store. Following Laterno's instruction, I observed the store to see if there were any violations of the campus policy. I understood how important it was to the University that there were no liquor violations at the store.

I positioned myself in the window of Miller's Deli and Coffee Shop directly across from the liquor store on Campus Drive. I began my surveillance at 6:00 p.m. From 6:00 p.m. until 8:00 p.m. there was a steady stream of customers entering the store. I did not observe anyone enter the store who appeared to be underage. There were two employees in the store, one of whom I later identified as Pat Rogers. At 7:45 p.m. the second employee left the store, as there appeared to be a lull in business. The second employee came over to Miller's Deli and Coffee Shop and had a free-range organic, all-natural turkey and sprout sandwich on whole wheat bread and a double latte with the house blend and double sugar.

At 8:00 p.m. I observed an older man walking from the east up the sidewalk on Campus Drive. The man appeared to be disheveled and unkempt. He was very unsteady on his feet. He was wearing a dirty blue work shirt, a red bandanna around his neck, and a pair of soiled, pleated khaki pants. He was wearing very dirty unlaced tennis shoes. (*If the climate in your area requires the wearing of a coat, add the following: Tolefson was wearing a dirty, blue, quilted ski jacket. Additionally, if it will be dark at this time of year, add the following: the area is well lit from lighting from adjacent stores and lights on the buildings that illuminate the sidewalk.*) I later learned this man was Erik Tolefson, a retired professor of Midstate University.

I watched Tolefson stagger to the door of the liquor store. He paused at the door for a few seconds and entered. He walked directly to the counter and stood in front of Rogers. I could not hear what they said, but I could see both of them clearly through the full, plate-glass window.

Tolefson did not stagger inside the store and was inside only for a short time. When he left, he was carrying a sack containing a bottle of GlenLucy single malt whisky and a receipt for the sale.

Tolefson was carrying a paper bag containing a receipt and a bottle of GlenLucy single malt whisky when he came out of the store. He was not carrying a bag when he entered the store. I then seized the bag from him. I took photographs of the receipt, the sack containing the whisky, and the bottle of GlenLucy.

I approached Mr. Tolefson and asked him if he had been drinking. He said, "You're darn tootin', my good fellow, and I suggest it isn't any business of yours." We discussed the weather, and I observed that Tolefson was slurred of speech, his breath smelled of alcohol, his eyes were bloodshot, and he was unsteady on his feet. I asked him to perform three field sobriety tests: 1) the walk-and-turn test—he staggered and nearly fell on turning; 2) the one-leg stand—he could not stand on one leg; and 3) Horizontal Gaze Nystagmus (HGN)—I held my index finger about a foot in front of Tolefson's eyes and asked Tolefson to follow my finger with his eyes. Tolefson failed the sobriety tests. I administered a Portable Breath Test (PBT) and determined he had a .12 percent blood alcohol concentration.

I asked Tolefson for some identification, and I noted that he fumbled for his wallet and had difficulty removing his driver's license. Tolefson dropped his license, and I picked it up for him. After recording Professor Tolefson's address, I permitted him to leave.

I then went into the Off Campus Liquor Store and talked to Pat Rogers. I identified myself and asked Rogers if Tolefson had purchased any alcohol in the store. Rogers replied, "Yes." Then I asked Rogers if Rogers had noticed Tolefson was drunk. Rogers said, "I have never met Tolefson before, and he did not look drunk to me. He looked like a tired old man who may have been sleeping rough and who had a cold."

I told Rogers that I would be making a report to the President of the University, and since I believed there was a violation of the Employment and Management of the Off Campus Liquor Store, Rule 6, I expected Rogers would be terminated.

I have attached the four photographs.

M. J. Troy

M. J. Troy, Chief of Police

11:30 p.m.

cc: D. Laterno, President Midstate University

Photograph of Tolefson's Receipt of Purchase from Off Campus Liquor Store

Off Campus Liquor Store
9191 Campus Drive
Silver Springs, Nita
555-555-5555

1L. GlenLucy Scotch Whisky	$42.99
SUBTOTAL	$42.99
@ 7% Sales Tax	$3.01
TOTAL	**$45.99**
Cash Tendered	$50.00
CHANGE	**$4.01**

Thank you for shopping at
Off Campus Liquor Store
Retain this Receipt for your Records

Date: Friday, _____ **(Week -6)**
Transaction Ref. Number: 5432-5273-0602
Salesperson: Pat

Photographs of Tolefson's Bottle of GlenLucy in Bag

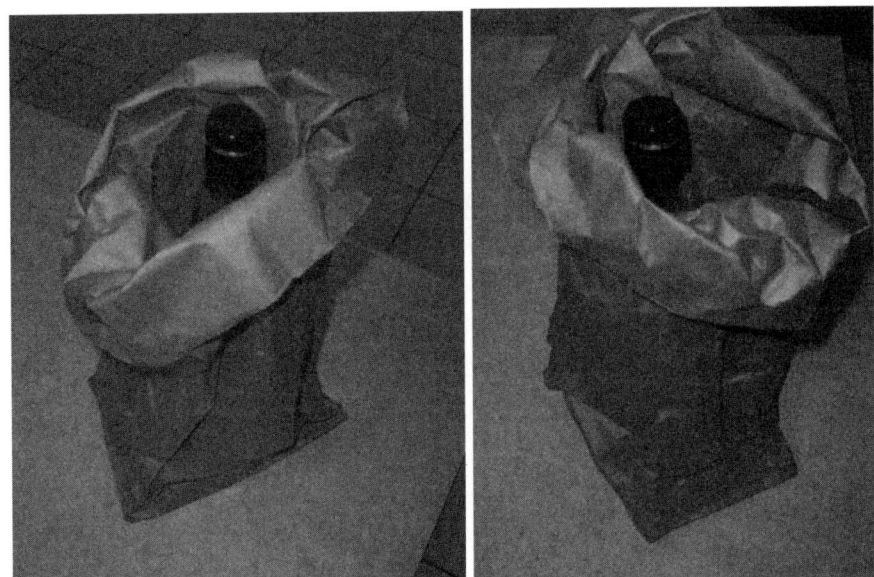

Photograph of Tolefson's Bottle of GlenLucy

Pat Rogers
7044 Balsam Trail
Silver Springs, Nita 55515
999-869-9053

_____ **(Monday, Week -5)**

President D. Laterno
Midstate University
10500 Campus Drive
Silver Springs, Nita 55515

Dear President Laterno,

Last Friday, University Chief of Police M. J. Troy came into the liquor store and told me I had sold liquor to an obviously intoxicated person and a report of the violation was going to you. Chief Troy was very rude to me. Troy told me that there had been rumors about sales to underage people and that the liquor store was under surveillance because there were rumors of liquor being sold to underage students. Troy told me I would probably be fired.

I did sell liquor to that old man. He looked to me to be a poor, tired old man. I thought he had been sleeping on the street and that he had a cold. I did see that his eyes were blood shot though I did not think he was drunk. He was in the store a short time, and I did not talk to him for very long. I was surprised he bought such an expensive bottle of whisky and paid cash for it.

This job means a lot to me. I love working for the University. I know all the Rules of Employment of the Off Campus Liquor Store and of the employment contract I signed. I would never knowingly break any rules. I sold my other businesses in order to work for Midstate University, and I am the only source of support for my two kids. The health benefits are very important to me. I hope you will not fire me.

Sincerely,

Pat Rogers

Pat Rogers

Midstate University

Office of the President

10500 Campus Drive

Silver Springs, Nita 55515

_____ **(Wednesday, Week -5)**

Pat Rogers

7044 Balsam Trail

Silver Springs, Nita 55515

Dear Pat Rogers,

I received a copy of Police Chief Troy's report dated Friday, _____**(Week -6)** and your letter to me dated the following Monday. Based on both documents, and after a full examination of the employment contract you signed and the Rules of Employment and Management of the Off Campus Liquor Store, specifically Rule 6, it is my unfortunate duty to inform you that you are immediately terminated as an employee of Midstate University. Your health benefits will continue for one month as of the date of this letter, and you have earned one sick day and one vacation day. Payment for your sick days and your vacation days will be added to your final paycheck, which will include your wages up to and including today.

Please clean out your office immediately upon receipt of this letter and vacate the premises!

If you wish to file a grievance, you have thirty (30) days in which to do so pursuant to Article 28 of the Collective Bargaining Agreement between SPEU and Midstate University. I have attached your employment records. If you wish to see Midstate University records on this matter, please contact Alex Margolis, the Human Resource Director, and a copy of the records will be provided to you without cost. The grievance will be heard by an arbitrator. If you elect to have the matter resolved by a trial rather than by arbitration, see the terms and conditions of the Collective Bargaining Agreement.

You may keep the original of this hand-delivered memorandum.

Please sign the copy of this letter so we can assure you have receipt of the notice of termination.

Sincerely,

Dr. D. Laterno

Dr. D. Laterno

I have received the original of this memorandum and understand I am immediately being terminated as an employee of Midstate University. I understand my rights to appeal this termination and submit the matter to binding arbitration, and I am aware I may choose to bypass arbitration and have the matter heard by a judge or jury under Article 28 of the Collective Bargaining Agreement between Midstate University and the State Professional Employee Union (SPEU).

Pat Rogers

Date: _____ **(Wednesday, Week -5)**

Pat Rogers

METROPOLITAN NEWS

L. Marie, Publisher—John Oliver, Editor

In the News:

City Council Reports "Open Door" Meetings Are Now Closed

Police Composite Picture of Bank Robber Wearing Ski Mask, Sun Glasses, and Lip Gloss to Be Released Soon

_____ **(Friday, Week -5)**

Liquor Store Manager Fired for Selling Booze

As predicted, the liquor store owned by the University got into trouble shortly after it began to operate under University management. Pat Rogers, the former operator of a chain of coffee and bagel shops who was hired to manage the liquor store, has been accused of selling liquor to an obviously intoxicated person. While Rogers had no prior experience in the liquor business, the University decided Rogers was the person for the job.

Midstate University Police Chief Troy said, "We heard all sorts of rumors about Rogers. We were informed that the store was poorly managed and was selling liquor to underage students and drunk people in violation of the employment contract and University policy. I conducted a stake-out and caught Rogers red handed."

A source close to University President D. Laterno told *Metropolitan News* that Laterno had learned Rogers deceived the University about qualifications when applying for the job and heard from liquor store employees that Rogers was a terrible manager. Rogers was fired for violating University rules. In addition, the source said that Rogers was a troublemaker and not a team player.

The source said the University was misled into making a horrible mistake by hiring a hippy, coffee house, counter-culture weirdo.

The Union has filed a grievance against the University, and it is expected there will be an arbitration or a trial to determine if the firing of Rogers was with just cause.

Under the Union contract, SPEU will represent Rogers if the matter goes to binding arbitration. The issue is whether the University had just cause to fire Rogers. If it did, the arbitrator can uphold the termination. If there was not just cause, the arbitrator can require the University to reinstate Rogers with back pay. The terms of the contract also permit Rogers to elect to have a trial with a judge or jury.

The *Metropolitan News* has confirmed that the University has already hired a replacement. "The contract we have here is unique. Rogers can seek damages for unlawful termination regardless of the outcome," a Union official declared. "However, a court battle could be long and hurtful for both Midstate University and Rogers."

STATE PROFESSIONAL EMPLOYEE UNION
SPEU

Local #1234

75 Central Avenue, Suite 200, Silver Springs, Nita 55515

GRIEVANCE FORM No. E-69   Date: _____ **(Monday, Week -4)**

Name of State Employer: *Midstate University*

Union Member's Name: *Pat Rogers*

Home Address: *7044 Balsam Trail*   Phone Number: *999.869.9053*

City: *Silver Springs*   State: *Nita*   Zip: **55515**

Type of Claim: ✓ **Discharge** __ Suspension __Pay Claim __ Seniority Violation __ Other

Description of Grievance

Contract Violation Alleged:

The discharge was in violation of the Collective Bargain Agreement, including but not limited to Article 28, Rule 6, Rules of Employment and Management of the Off Campus Liquor Store.

Specific Facts of Contract Violation:

Employer alleges Employee Rogers, while employed as a manager of the Off Campus Liquor Store, knowingly sold alcohol to an intoxicated person on _____**(Friday, Week -6)**. Employer alleges this is a violation of a critical work rule under Article 28, B1, of the Collective Bargaining Agreement.

Employee denies these allegations.

Relief Sought:

Reinstatement with full back pay, job classification prior to discharge, and all other appropriate relief.

Article of Contract Violated: *Collective Bargaining Agreement, Article 28, and Rules of Employment and Management of the Off Campus Liquor Store, Rule 6*

Action Requested: *Reinstatement of job, with back pay and classification prior to discharge.*

Member: *Pat Rogers*   Steward: *Margaret Harmon*   Management: *D. Laterno*

This form is the sole possession of SPEU Local #1234. Only an authorized representative
of SPEU Local #1234 has the right to withdraw or settle this grievance.

Pat Rogers
7044 Balsam Trail
Silver Springs, Nita 55515
999-869-9053

_____ **(Tuesday, Week -4)**

Dr. D. Laterno
President
Midstate University
10500 Campus Drive
Silver Springs, Nita 55515

Dear President Laterno,

I cannot begin to tell you how furious I am. You have taken away my job, my kids' future, and now my good name. I realize now that my hopes for a new life were just dreams. I was cheated by you and the University. I gave up a $60,000 job and sold my businesses because the University wanted me to go to work immediately, and I could not run the businesses and work for the University at the same time. I was able to sell my company and pay off my debts. I was also able to terminate the leases for my shop for $10,000. I will never be able to restart the shops because a large chain of stores has recently moved into the area where my shops were located.

I planned for my kids to attend the University elementary, high school, and eventually Midstate University itself. The three-quarter tuition waiver was a wonderful benefit for me and my kids; I could never afford the $5,000 grade school; $10,000 high school; and $20,000 college tuition otherwise. You took away our hopes. I now have no health care or retirement fund.

To add insult to injury, your office said those horrible things about me to the newspaper. I am referring to the *Metropolitan News* article dated _____**(Friday, Week -5)**. I have never been careless about my job. I never sold alcohol to any underage students nor have any of the employees. I have never done anything against the University and received only positive reviews from you as an employee. You never even gave me a chance.

How can you live with yourself? I cannot sleep, and my kids are under terrible stress. I cannot make my house payment or even buy food. I am desperate.

I have contacted an attorney and hereby inform you under Article 28 of the Collective Bargaining Agreement between Midstate University and the State Professional Employee Union (SPEU), I am electing to bypass arbitration and have this matter heard by a judge or jury in a trial. My attorney advised me to inform you that a complaint in this matter will be forthcoming.

Sincerely,

Pat Rogers

Pat Rogers

Midstate University

Office of the President

10500 Campus Drive

Silver Springs, Nita 55515

_____ **(Friday, Week -4)**

Pat Rogers
7044 Balsam Trail
Silver Springs, Nita 55515

Dear Pat Rogers,

I am in receipt of your most recent letter. No one from Midstate University was authorized to make any of the statements in the *Metropolitan News* article you sent me dated _____**(Friday, Week -5)**. No one in my office or from the University said any of the things quoted by the *Metropolitan News*. I never made any of those statements attributed to me. You were terminated for one reason, for violating Rule 6 of the Rules of Employment and Management of the Off Campus Liquor Store—knowingly selling alcohol to an obviously intoxicated person.

I contacted our attorneys and informed them you have elected to bypass arbitration under the terms of the Collective Bargaining Agreement between Midstate University and the State Professional Employee Union (SPEU) and that you elected to have the matter heard at a court or jury trial.

Sincerely,

Dr. D. Laterno

Dr. D. Laterno
President
Midstate University

MIDSTATE UNIVERSITY POLICE

FOLLOW-UP REPORT

_____ **(Day - 10)**

Follow-Up Report

TO: The File

FROM: Police Chief M. J. Troy

Acting on the advice of the advocate representing Midstate University, I am providing this follow-up report concerning the incident at the Off Campus Liquor Store on _____ **(Friday, Week -6)**. This report is based on my field notes that I have discarded.

When I first saw Professor Tolefson, I paid particular attention to him. I immediately thought he was drunk and assumed he was heading into the liquor store. I thought if Tolefson bought a bottle of liquor at the Off Campus Liquor Store, it would be a violation of the Rules of Employment and Management of the Off Campus Liquor Store, Rule 6. That is the type of situation that President Laterno worried about.

After Professor Tolefson went into the store, he seemed to pull himself together and walked straight to the counter. I observed exactly where he stood. He was directly across from Pat Rogers. I briefly met Rogers once at a training session.

Three days after the incident I measured the width of the counter. It was thirty inches wide. Tolefson appeared to be standing right up against the counter, and Rogers was about six inches from the back of the counter.

I timed exactly how long Tolefson and Rogers faced each other. I used the second hand on my watch and observed they faced each other for sixty-six seconds. After that, Rogers turned around and was busy getting a bottle from the shelf and putting it in a package.

Starting at the time Rogers rang up the sale until Tolefson turned and left the store, the time elapsed was ninety-five seconds. Rogers and Tolefson were facing each other for sixty-six seconds of this time with the cash register between them. I could see Rogers's lips move, and occasionally from the side I could see Tolefson's lips move, too. Of course I could not hear what either of them said. From where I watched, they were about seventy feet away from me.

I did not see Tolefson stumble or stagger inside the store. I have attached to this report a diagram that I recently prepared. It shows the path of Professor Tolefson. While it is not to scale, it is accurate.

When the professor came out of the store, I seized a sack that contained the bottle of GlenLucy whisky and the receipt for the sale. The photographs of the receipt, the bottle in the sack, and the bottle of GlenLucy whisky are accurate.

Inside the store the light was good, there was some soft music playing, and there were no smells. Outside the store there was a slight breeze blowing and some traffic noise. I placed myself directly in front of Tolefson so I could be in the same position but further away than Rogers was inside the store. I also observed Tolefson for less time than Rogers did. Placing myself in the suspect's position is very important. After my observations, I administered the field sobriety and breathalyzer test to Tolefson.

I have received a great deal of training in alcohol enforcement. I was a street officer for two years in Portland, West-State, and a police officer on the force at Midstate University for ten years before I became Chief of Police for Midstate University. I train my officers in alcohol enforcement because it is important to the University. I have written two articles about alcohol violations: "Spotting the Drunk Driver" and "Drinking Yourself to Death." Both were published in the *National Police Officers Magazine* within the last two years.

I did not include this much detail in my original report as I usually use the report only to refresh my recollection of events. I write an average of two reports a day and perform a lot of administrative work. I have an excellent memory of this event.

From a distance of four feet I could see the following:

Appearance of the professor

- Hair dirty and matted (there was a dead leaf with a small twig in his hair)
- Clothes filthy—dirt stains, torn pants at the knee, food stains on the blue work shirt
- Eyes very bloodshot—could not see the whites as they were very red
- Eyes glassy and pupils dilated
- Wet greenish matter in the corners of his eyes and caked matter under his eyes
- Nose very red and running
- Tolefson licked the moisture from his upper lip twice as I stood in front of him
- Beard stubble
- Wet trousers—medium-sized wet stain at crotch—smelled of urine
- Dirty tennis shoes, untied

Smell

- Very strong smell of alcohol coming from his breath
- Body odor
- Dirt/earth smell
- Urine smell

Rogers v. Midstate Univ.—Trial

Stance

- Swayed a few inches back and forth the whole time he was in front of me—I could not see this sway from where I was watching him inside the store—it appeared he could control it inside

- Feet spread wider apart than normal

- Fumbling for identification while he was getting out driver's license

Speech

- Very slurred—difficult to understand

- Tolefson did tell me (with difficulty) that he had been gardening in his year-round greenhouse, and when he finished he had some drinks. He said his wife was out of town, so he decided to get what he called a "snoot full." He said he drank single malt whisky. I asked him if he knew he had wet his pants, and he said, "Of course, you fool! Do you think I am completely out of control?" He said he had two cups of coffee and the whisky before leaving home, and when he walked halfway to the liquor store he had to "make water." He said something about his "gol-darned" prostate. He tried to get to the store to use the toilet, but didn't make it. He said it was one of the problems of getting old.

I instructed the training sessions concerning the University's alcohol and drug policies and the workshop on identifying people under the influence and methods to deal with them. My records show that Rogers attended the policy session, although I have no recollection of Rogers's presence. The class had about forty people in it.

I do remember Rogers at the next session, which was the workshop on spotting intoxicated people. I told the students to turn off their cell phones as I think it is rude when they ring in class. As the class started, Rogers's phone rang. I was irritated. Rogers interrupted the class and said, "I have to leave. My child is ill." I told Rogers I understood the problem. Rogers apologized for the phone call and missing the class. We agreed the class could be made up the next time it was offered. However, the class was not offered again before Rogers was fired.

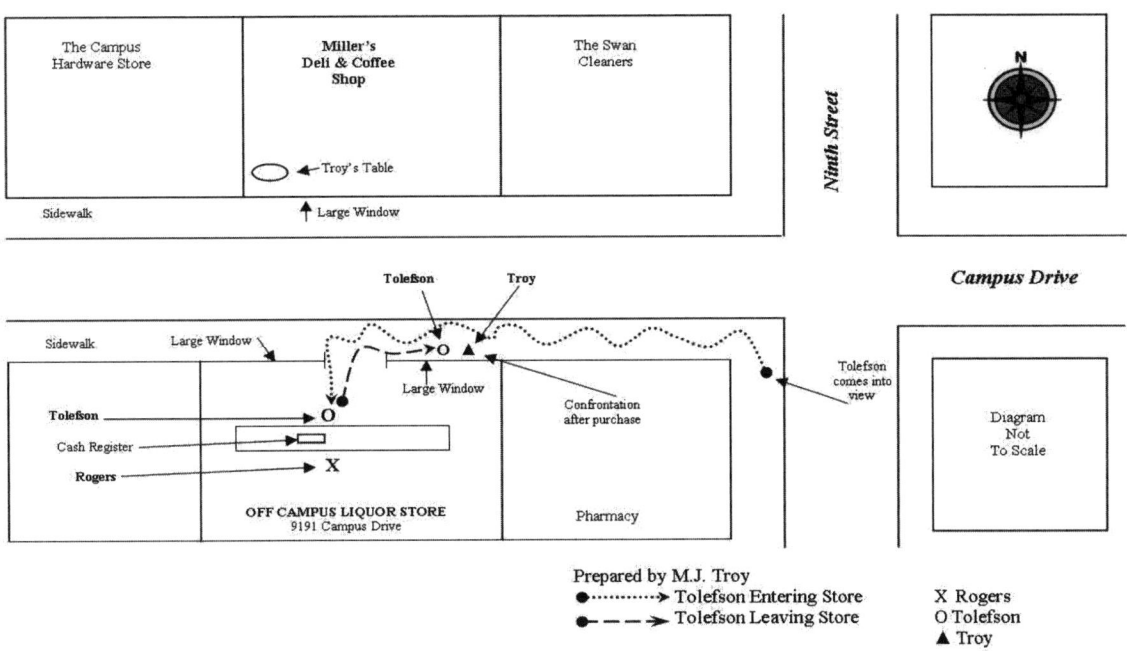

Follow-Up Incident Diagram—Prepared by M. J. Troy, _____**(Day -10)**

Pat Rogers
7044 Balsam Trail
Silver Springs, Nita 55515
999-869-9053

_____ **(Day -9)**

Union Advocate Representing Pat Rogers
75 Spring Hill Drive
Northfield, Nita

Dear Advocate,

After I met with someone in your office last week (I do not remember the person's name) I thought a lot about what happened the day I sold the bottle of GlenLucy whisky to the old man. I had been working very hard all day and was really tired. My children were sick the night before, and I was worried about them. I gave the other clerk a break when there was a lull in business. That is when the old man came in. I did not see the man outside the store before he came in. I saw the man as he walked right to the counter. He did not stand real close to the counter, but was about four feet from where I was. He did not say much. All I heard him say was, "Hey there, young one, I'd like to buy a liter of GlenLucy." That is all he said. He had a strange accent that I could not define.

I noticed he looked really tired and was dirty. His eyes looked bloodshot, and he looked like he had a head cold. His hair was unkempt, and he had on a blue work shirt *(add blue ski jacket if climate requires)*. I also saw he had a red bandanna around his neck. I did not pay any attention to his pants or shoes. We occasionally get a homeless person into the store. These poor people often live on the street. I do not think I should refuse them the right to buy liquor just because they might be poor and homeless. This is why I was surprised the man bought GlenLucy. I turned to get the bottle from the shelf behind me and put the bottle in a brown paper bag. When I turned around the man had placed a $50 bill on the counter. I rang up the sale, put the receipt into the bag, and gave the change to the man. He held his hand out for it and put the change in his pocket. When I gave him the change I noticed his hand had a small tremor in it. He took the bottle of whisky, said thank you, and walked out of the store. He was in the store a very short time. I'm not sure how long, but no more than a couple of minutes.

He did not stumble or stagger inside the store. The man did not slur his speech when he talked to me, and except for the strange accent I did not notice anything odd about how he spoke. I did not smell alcohol on his breath. He did smell like body odor and dirt. When he left, I saw the person talking to him. I learned later it was the Chief of Police, Troy. I thought they were friends, as they were both kind of waving their arms and talking. I didn't pay any further attention to them after a few seconds. Before the other clerk left for break, he had broken a bottle of Canadian whisky and had not completely cleaned it up before he left. There was a strong smell from the broken bottle, which was about five feet behind the counter. I mopped up the spill after Tolefson left and before Chief Troy came into the store.

I was really surprised when Chief Troy confronted me. I couldn't believe it. I have done a good job for the University. Neither I nor anyone else in the store has broken any laws or violated any of the Rules of Employment and Management of the Off Campus Liquor Store. I know the liquor store is controversial and would not do anything to jeopardize my job or the University. I attended all but one of the three-hour monthly training programs after I was hired. The fourth program was about the problems of on-campus alcohol and drug use and explained the policies of the University. It was a good session conducted by Chief Troy and was very clear. Session five was supposed to cover identifying people who were under the influence of alcohol and drugs. We were going to have a workshop and see a film. Just as the session was about to begin, my cell phone rang. (I was embarrassed, and Police Chief Troy was upset by the interruption.) My fourteen-year-old babysitter called and said my youngest child was vomiting, and I had to go home. I told Chief Troy, and I agreed to attend the session the next time it was offered. It was not offered again before I was fired.

I am proud of the job I have done for the University and the fact that revenues are going to a program I feel strongly about. When the funding for programs was stopped and the affirmative action programs were decreased, many young people were denied an opportunity they deserved.

The University provided some training, but I had to leave early because of a family situation. I had a good reason to leave and informed the instructor. When I ran my own business I was fair to everyone. Every employee had an equal shot with me. If a person had potential, I provided them training. I am a really good manager. I am not much of a drinker and have not had sufficient training in spotting people who have been drinking except for the University training I already mentioned above. The University never followed up with training. I am an employee doing the best job I can.

The University is using me as a scapegoat. They are embarrassed about owning a liquor store. There is nothing illegal about selling liquor to people over the age of twenty-one. The key is for people not to abuse it.

Why doesn't the University have the courage to stand up for a good employee like me instead of sneaking around "investigating"? I am bitter and angry. I need this job and the benefits it provides for me and my children. I think the University and Chief Troy are out to get me.

I know you will do an excellent job representing me and that you will teach the University a lesson they will never forget.

Sincerely,

Pat Rogers

Pat Rogers
cc: D. Laterno

Midstate University

10500 Campus Drive

Silver Springs, Nita

_____ **(Day -8)**

TO: Law Firm Representing Midstate University
FROM: The Office of the President
           Midstate University
           Dr. D. Laterno, President
CC: M. J. Troy, Alex Margolis, P. T. Ferguson, and Pat Rogers
RE: Termination of Pat Rogers for just cause

On Wednesday, ____**(Week -5)**, after an examination of all the records and files in this matter, I made the decision to terminate Pat Rogers as an employee of Midstate University. I do not normally become involved in personnel decisions, but I did so this time because of the unique and serious circumstances surrounding this incident.

Approximately one year ago, the University was granted a liquor store located near the campus of the University as a gift. This unique gift was provided by Mr. and Mrs. Wong, graduates of the University. They gave the gift because they felt the University was responsible for giving them an opportunity for an education and for their subsequent business success. This gift was particularly important to the University since Midstate University has been under considerable financial pressure for the last five years. The legislature has continually reduced funding, and many programs have been cut, particularly programs for assisting minority persons competing successfully and completing University studies. The Off Campus Liquor Store has an annual net return of at least one million dollars. With the gift of the liquor store, the Wongs set two rules: 1) the liquor store could not be sold; and 2) the annual proceeds must be spent to develop or continue programs to assist minority persons to compete and successfully complete a University education. The importance of the gift cannot be understated because of the cuts to affirmative action programs and the terminations of these programs due to lack of funding. This gift, however, was very controversial.

Over the last five years, use of alcohol by underaged students on campuses throughout the state, at both public and private schools, has reached serious levels. There have been three student deaths in the state attributed to alcohol. Binge drinking has become a serious problem, and the University has passed strict rules about the use of alcohol on campus and by underaged persons. The newspaper, as well as some legislators, have been critical of the University's acceptance of the gift and the conditions. One headline read: "University Sells Soul for Alcohol Money."

Nevertheless, I made the decision to accept the gift. I believed that strict management rules could prevent abuse or problems at the liquor store. I worked with the University attorney to develop the Rules of Employment and Management of the Off Campus Liquor Store:

Rule 6: Sale of Alcohol to Minors or Intoxicated Persons

- No alcohol will be sold to an underage person.

- Employees are required to obtain identification of anyone who is not clearly of a legal age.

- No alcohol can knowingly be sold to a person who is intoxicated.

  - Intoxicated is defined to mean anyone over .08 percent blood alcohol.

  - Knowingly is defined as: knowing or should have known the buyer was intoxicated.

- A violation of any provision of Rule 6 is a violation of a Critical Work Rule under Article 28, B(1) of the Collective Bargaining Agreement (CBA), and the employee is subject to immediate termination.

- An employee terminated under the provision of Rule 6 and Article 28 of the Collective Bargaining Agreement (CBA) will lose all University benefits except for accrued and vested retirement funds.

Approximately nine months ago, the University hired Pat Rogers through its normal procedure. I read Rogers's application and job reviews prepared by Alex Margolis, the Midstate University Director of Personnel.

I read in Pat Rogers's application and resume an admission of being well aware of the controversy surrounding the gift of the liquor store to the University. Rogers expressed concern about the abuse of alcohol by young people and the problems of alcohol abuse on campuses. Rogers went on to say that the gift provides vital resources and that with careful management and close attention to standards and rules, the liquor store can be run appropriately and will not become a liability.

About two months ago, I heard rumors that alcohol was being sold to underage students at the Off Campus Liquor Store. On Thursday, _____ **(Week -6)**, I met with Chief of Police, M. J. Troy, and discussed the problem with Troy. I instructed Troy to observe the liquor store and see if there were any violations of the campus policy.

On Saturday, _____ **(Week -6)**, Chief Troy personally provided me with a report of the occurrences of the previous day at the liquor store, which stated that alcohol had been sold by Pat Rogers to an obviously intoxicated person. At my home on Saturday, _____ **(Week -6)**, I discussed the matter with Chief Troy at length. I was provided with significant details concerning the sale of alcohol to the intoxicated person.

On Monday, _____ **(Week -5)**, I received a letter from Pat Rogers providing a justification for the sale of alcohol to the intoxicated person.

I have examined the Rules of Employment and Management of the Off Campus Liquor Store, particularly Rule 6 stated above.

Normally employee discipline follows a four-step process, with progressive discipline implemented by our Personnel Department. First there is an oral reprimand; 2) a written reprimand; 3) a written reprimand with suspension not to exceed four work weeks; and 4) a written reprimand and termination. However, because of the special circumstances surrounding the Off Campus Liquor Store, particular rules were developed for employment and management of that liquor store. Because of the seriousness of this violation, sale of alcohol to an underaged person, or to an intoxicated person, demanded immediate termination without the steps of progressive discipline.

After a full review of the files, a complete understanding of Pat Rogers's employment records and the circumstances surrounding the sale of alcohol to an intoxicated person, I decided to terminate Pat Rogers for just cause under Rule 6 of the Rules of Employment and Management of the Off Campus Liquor Store.

A letter of termination was dated Wednesday, _____**(Week -5)**, and was received and signed by Pat Rogers on Wednesday, _____**(Week -5)**.

On Tuesday, _____**(Week -4)**, I received a letter from Pat Rogers complaining about the termination and also including statements allegedly made by persons from my office to the *Metropolitan News* newspaper. After receiving Rogers's letter, I wrote a return letter on Friday, _____**(Week -4),** in which I denied that anyone from my office made statements to the paper. However, on Friday, _____**(Week -3)**, I learned that the information provided to the newspaper was provided by my administrative assistant, John Marden. It was improper for Marden to make those off-the-record statements to the newspaper. I accepted John Marden's resignation that day, and Marden is no longer employed by the University.

Sincerely,

Dr. D. Laterno

Dr. D. Laterno
President
Midstate University

Pat Rogers
7044 Balsam Trail
Silver Springs, Nita 55515
999-869-9053

_____ **(Day -9)**

Dr. D. Laterno
President
Midstate University
10500 Campus Drive
Silver Springs, Nita 55515

Dear President Laterno,

   Under the Collective Bargaining Agreement between Midstate University and the State Public Employees Union, Article 28(E), I hereby notify you and Midstate University that I am electing to have the matter of my termination heard at a trial. I choose not to have an arbitration in this matter. I understand that my attorney, Ms. Gena Robins, has filed a summons and complaint in this matter.

Sincerely,

Pat Rogers

Pat Rogers

PLEADINGS

STATE OF NITA

COUNTY OF DARROW

DISTRICT COURT

SECOND JUDICIAL DISTRICT

Court File No. 5431

PAT ROGERS,

   Plaintiff,

v.

SUMMONS

MIDSTATE UNIVERSITY,

   Defendant.

THE STATE OF NITA TO THE ABOVE-NAMED DEFENDANT:

  YOU ARE HEREBY SUMMONED and required to serve upon Plaintiff's attorneys an Answer to the Complaint, which is herewith served upon you, within twenty (20) days after service of the Summons upon you, exclusive of the day of service. If you fail to do so, judgment by default will be taken against you for the relief demanded in the Complaint.

Date: _____**(Monday, Week -3)**

Gena Robins

Gena Robins
Attorney for Plaintiff

STATE OF NITA   **DISTRICT COURT**

COUNTY OF DARROW   **SECOND JUDICIAL DISTRICT**

PAT ROGERS,

           Plaintiff,

    v.   **COMPLAINT**

MIDSTATE UNIVERSITY,

           Defendant.

Plaintiff, Pat Rogers claims relief, states and alleges as follows:

A. PARTIES AND JURISDICTION AND VENUE

1. Pat Rogers is an individual residing at 7044 Balsam Trail, Silver Springs, State of Nita.

2. Midstate University, is a legal entity doing business at 10500 Campus Drive, Silver Springs, State of Nita.

3. The events in question occurred solely with the boundaries of the State of Nita.

B. COUNTS

1. On _____ **(Last Thursday, Month -11)**, Plaintiff was offered and accepted employment as the store manager at the Off Campus Liquor Store owned by Defendant.

2. Prior to accepting employment from Defendant, Plaintiff's salary was $60,000 annually and Plaintiff was the owner of a business.

3. On _____ **(First Monday, Month -3)**, Defendant conducted a six-month review of Plaintiff's work performance and highly recommended retention.

4. Plaintiff's employment compensation package included an annual salary of $55,000, full health and dental coverage for Plaintiff and Plaintiff's legal dependants, and a vested retirement after a six-month probationary period. These benefits are worth 33 1/3 percent of employee's salary. Additional benefits include three-quarters tuition waiver for children's elementary school attendance (full tuition is $5,000 annually), three-quarters tuition waiver for children's high school education (full tuition is $10,000 annually), and three-quarters tuition waiver for qualified enrollment at Midstate University (full tuition is $20,000 annually).

5. On _____ **(Wednesday, Week -5)**, Plaintiff was wrongfully terminated.

6. Defendant's conduct was in violation of the termination procedures of the Collective Bargaining Agreement and Rogers's terms of employment for the following reasons:

    a. Plaintiff did not violate the terms of the Collective Bargaining Agreement or the terms of employment.

    b. Plaintiff did not intentionally and knowingly sell alcohol to an intoxicated person.

7. As a direct and proximate result of Defendant's wrongful termination of Plaintiff, Plaintiff has in the past and will in the future suffer the following damages—loss of earnings and earning capacity; medical and dental insurance costs; educational tuition waivers for Plaintiff's children from their elementary through post-secondary educations; and pension and retirement benefits— all in an amount greater than fifty thousand dollars ($50,000).

WHEREFORE, Plaintiff prays that:

1. Judgment in an amount in excess of fifty-thousand dollars ($50,000.00).

2. For all other relief this Court deems equitable and just.

Dated: _____ **(Monday, Week -3)**

Gena Robins

Gena Robins
Attorney for Plaintiff

ACKNOWLEDGMENT

The undersigned hereby acknowledges that costs, disbursements, and reasonable attorney and witness fees may be awarded to the opposing party or parties in this litigation if the Court should find that the undersigned acted in bad faith, asserted a claim or defense that is frivolous and that is costly to the other party, asserted an unfounded position solely to delay the ordinary course of the proceedings or to harass, or committed fraud upon the Court.

Dated: _____ **(Monday, Week -3)**

Gena Robins

Gena Robins
Attorney for Plaintiff

STATE OF NITA

COUNTY OF DARROW

DISTRICT COURT

SECOND JUDICIAL DISTRICT

PAT ROGERS,

        Plaintiff,

v.

MIDSTATE UNIVERSITY,

        Defendant.

ANSWER

Defendant, Midstate University, (Defendant) for its Answer to Plaintiff's Complaint states and alleges as follows:

GENERAL DENIAL

1. Denies each and every allegation, matter, statement, and thing contained in the Plaintiff's Complaint and puts Plaintiff to its strict burden of proof, save and except as hereinafter expressly admitted, qualified, or otherwise answered.

A. PARTIES AND JURISDICTION

Upon information and belief, Defendant admits the allegations contained in paragraphs A1, A2, and A3 of Plaintiff's Complaint.

B. COUNTS

1. Upon information and belief, Defendant admits the allegation contained in paragraph B1 of Plaintiff's Complaint.

2. Upon information and belief, Defendant admits the allegation contained in paragraph B2 of Plaintiff's Complaint.

3. Upon information and belief, Defendant admits the allegation contained in paragraph B3 of Plaintiff's Complaint.

4. Upon information and belief, Defendant admits the allegation contained in paragraph B4 of Plaintiff's Complaint.

5. Upon information and belief, Defendant denies the allegation contained in paragraph B5 of Plaintiff's Complaint.

6. Upon information and belief, Defendant denies the allegation contained in paragraph B6 of Plaintiff's Complaint.

7. Upon information and belief, Defendant denies the allegation contained in paragraph B7 of Plaintiff's Complaint.

WHEREFORE, Defendant, Midstate University, prays that Rogers take nothing from Plaintiff's stated cause of action, and such other relief as the court deems proper.

Dated: _____ **(Wednesday, Week -3)**

James Garner

James Garner
Attorney for Defendant,
Midstate University

ACKNOWLEDGMENT

The undersigned hereby acknowledges that costs, disbursements and reasonable attorney and witness fees may be awarded to the opposing party or parties in this litigation if the Court should find that the undersigned acted in bad faith, asserted a claim or defense that is frivolous and that is costly to the other party, asserted an unfounded position solely to delay the ordinary course of the proceedings or to harass, or committed fraud upon the Court.

Dated: _____ **(Wednesday, Week -3)**

James Garner

James Garner
Attorney for Defendant,
Midstate University

Rogers v. Midstate Univ.—Trial

APPENDICES

APPENDIX A

DIRECTIONS

Burden of Proof

Court or Jury Trial

In a court or jury trial, the plaintiff shall have the burden of proof by a preponderance of the evidence.

Order of Presentation and Rules of Evidence

Court or Jury Trial (See Collective Bargaining Agreement Article 28)

- Pat Rogers is the Plaintiff (Employee), and Midstate University is the defendant.
- The Plaintiff must present evidence first.
- The Plaintiff may not call Defendant or defense witnesses in its case-in-chief.
- Local rules governing the order of opening statement and final argument:

    Option 1: The Plaintiff shall present the first opening statement and the concluding final argument. The Defendant shall not have a rebuttal final argument.

    Option 2: The Plaintiff shall present the first opening statement. The Plaintiff shall present the first final argument followed by the Defendant. The Plaintiff shall have a rebuttal final argument.

- The rules of evidence, procedure, and law of the jurisdiction where the complaint is filed shall govern, but shall not amend any terms of the agreement. The parties may also agree to use the Federal Rules of Evidence.

Suggested Time Schedule

The following schedule indicates how the time may be allocated. The time available for opening statement, witness examination, and final argument may be allocated as the attorneys wish. Objections and arguments will be counted against the attorney that is speaking.

Court Trial—Three Hours

Each side has sixty minutes available and will be responsible for keeping track of its time. The trial may take less time; however, the time should not exceed three hours.

Preliminary Discussion	**10 minutes**	
Plaintiff	**60 minutes***	
Defendant	**60 minutes†**	
Critique	**30 minutes**	
Breaks	**20 minutes**	
*	Opening statement	5 minutes
	Direct examination	30 minutes
	Cross-examination	15 minutes
	Final argument	10 minutes
†	Opening statement	5 minutes
	Direct examination	15 minutes
	Cross-examination	30 minutes
	Final argument	10 minutes

Jury Trial—Six Hours, Fifteen minutes

Each side has ninety minutes, plus ten minutes for jury selection. The trial may take less time; however, the total time should not exceed six hours and fifteen minutes.

Preliminary Discussion	**30 minutes**
Judge's Introduction	**10 minutes**
Jury Selection	**20 minutes (10 minutes per side)**
Plaintiff	**90 minutes***
Defendant	**90 minutes†**
Judge's Final Instructions	**10 minutes**
Jury Deliberation	**30 minutes**
Critique by Jury	**15 minutes**
Critique by Judge	**30 minutes**
Breaks	**20 minutes**
Lunch	**30 minutes**

*	Opening statement	10 minutes
	Direct examination	25 minutes
	Cross-examination	40 minutes
	Final argument	15 minutes
†	Opening statement	10 minutes
	Direct examination	40 minutes
	Cross-examination	25 minutes
	Final argument	15 minutes

Expert Witnesses

Expert witnesses are only called when expert witness examination is part of the exercise. Each expert witness examination adds thirty minutes per side (twenty minutes for direct examination and ten for cross-examination).

When expert witness examinations *are* a part of the exercise, the admissibility and use of expert witness reports are governed by the agreed-upon rules of evidence.

When expert examinations *are not* part of the exercise, the reports of the expert witnesses *are* admissible. The expert reports should be marked as exhibits and entered into evidence before opening statements. Both parties may refer to the reports in opening statement and final argument. In a trial, the judge *may* provide the report to the jury.

Negotiation and Mediation

The time schedules for negotiation and mediation exercises will be determined by faculty.

Rogers v. Midstate Univ.—Trial

APPENDIX B

SOME JUST CAUSE DEFINITIONS

SOME JUST CAUSE DEFINITIONS

(Examine your own jurisdictions's case law and statutes for definitions of just cause.)

The Supreme Court of the United States decided in 1960 that an arbitrator "does not sit to dispense his own brand of industrial justice." One of the court's most liberal jurists, William O. Douglas, wrote:

> [A]n arbitrator is confined to interpretation of the collective bargaining agreement; he does not dispense his own brand of industrial justice. He may of course look for guidance from many sources, yet his award is legitimate only so long as it draws its essence from the collective bargaining agreement. When the arbitrator's words manifest an infidelity to this obligation, courts have no choice but to refuse enforcement.

Steelworkers v. Enterprise Wheel & Car Corp., 463 Nita 2d 299 **(Year -46)**.

Prof. Edgar A. Jones Jr., a respected labor arbitrator, carefully questioned Justice Douglas:

> [A]ny arbitrator who has looked down the long corridor of his conscience at a "just cause" disciplinary grievance is apt to feel that, at best, it is pious sentiment, and, at worst, that it obscures and encumbers the abrasive necessity of pulling all of the elements of decision, including whatever biases he may experience, down into plain view. The parties in the "just cause" provision have conferred upon management the discretion to discipline the employees, but only for "just cause." Can it be said that the arbitrator does not sit to dispense his own brand of justice in that case? At that point, what other brand could there possibly be? Perhaps it is thought that it is necessary to the preservation of the acceptability of the arbitral process to enshroud it with a Delphic mystique. Assuming it was desirable (which it is not), does anyone really think it can be done?

11 *UCLA L. Rev.* 675, 764 (1964).

Almost twenty years later, Prof. Jones reached a slightly different conclusion, but made the same point that arbitrators are chosen for their brand of industrial justice:

> If the arbitrator in these cases "does not sit to dispense his own brand of industrial justice," what other brand is available for him to dispense? The standard answer is "that of the parties." If that be so, where does the arbitrator locate the parties' brand of justice when they have not set it out in the agreement?
>
> It would be astonishing if employers and unions did not pay considerable attention to the personal characteristics of the individual whom they select from the pack of available brands of industrial justice. This scrutiny by the collective bargainers is far from casual, particularly when lawyers are involved. The selection of an arbitrator is seen as central to the tactical problem of getting a favorable decision.

30 *UCLA L. Rev.* 881, 886, 889 (1983).

The following discussion covers the various definitions of just cause that have been developed, with particular attention on those arbitrators who are active.

Fundamental Understanding of the
Employment Relationship

Roger I. Abrams and Dennis R. Nolan are law professors and arbitrators. In their law review article (1985 *Duke L.J.* 594), they conclude that a true definition of just cause does not exist.

> Just cause is hardly an obvious concept. When applying it to specific cases, arbitrators tend to define just cause in nebulous terms or to make conclusory statements. For example, "reasonable" discipline is permissible[3] but "arbitrary," "excessive," or "discriminatory," discipline is not.[4] A penalty that does not "shock the conscience" of the arbitrator is upheld,[5] but one that is not "just" under "all the circumstances" is set aside.[6] In fact, one arbitrator characterized the term "just cause" as "purposefully ambiguous."[7] Although some arbitrators have identified various procedural prerequisites for just cause, even they have failed to base their proposals on a comprehensive theory of employee discipline.

> Leaving the determination of just cause to the discretion of effectively unreviewable arbitrators leads to inexplicable results. . . . Such decisions fail to serve the interests of either management or labor. They provide neither guidance for future conduct nor persuasive rationales. A systematic model of just cause is needed to guide employers and employees in their day-to-day conduct and to assist arbitrators in resolving disciplinary matters.

Hence, they propound a theory of just cause that seems based on an economic model:

A. Just cause for discipline exists only when an employee has failed to meet his obligations under the fundamental understanding of the employment relationship. The employee's general obligation is to provide satisfactory work. Satisfactory work has four components:

1. Regular Attendance.

2. Obedience to reasonable work rules.

3. A reasonable quality and quantity of work.

4. Avoidance of conduct, either at or away from work, which would interfere with the employer's ability to carry on the business effectively.

B. For there to be just cause, the discipline must further one or more of management's three legitimate interests:

---

[3] *See 3M Co.*, 80 Lab. Arb. (BNA) 926, 928 (1983)(Gallagher, Arb.); *Napoleon Bd. of Educ.*, 74 Lab. Arb. (BNA) 303, 305 (1980)(Roumell, Arb.); *Riley Stoker Corp.*, 7 Lab. Arb. (BNA) 764, 768 (1947)(Platt, Arb.).

[4] *See United States Sugar Corp.*, 82 Lab. Arb. (BNA) 604, 609 (1984)(Hanes, Arb.); *Kansas City Area Transp. Auth.*, 82 Lab. Arb. (BNA) 409, 413 (1984)(Maniscalco, Arb.); *Atlantic Richfield Co.*, 69 Lab. Arb. (BNA) 484, 487 (1977)(Sisk, Arb.).

[5] *See Monarch Mach. Tool Co.*, 82 Lab. Arb. (BNA) 880, 883 (1984)(Schedler, Arb.).

[6] *See City of Kalamazoo*, 82 Lab. Arb. (BNA) 138, 149-41 (1983)(Ellman, Arb.).

[7] *Municipality of Anchorage*, 82 Lab. Arb. (BNA) 256, 263 (1983)(Hauck, Arb.).

Rogers v. Midstate Univ.—Trial

1. Rehabilitation of a potentially satisfactory employee.

2. Deterrence of similar conduct, either by the disciplined employee or other employees.

3. Protection of the employer's ability to operate the business successfully.

C. The concept of just cause includes certain employee protections that reflect the union's interest in guaranteeing "fairness" in disciplinary situations.

    1. The employee is entitled to *industrial due process.* This includes:

        a. actual or constructive notice of expected standards of conduct and penalties for wrongful conduct.

        b. a decision based on facts, determined after an investigation that provides the employee an opportunity to state his case, with union assistance if he desires it.

        c. the imposition of discipline in gradually increasing degrees, except in cases involving the most extreme breaches of the fundamental understanding. In particular, discharge may be imposed only when less severe penalties will not protect legitimate management interests, for one of the following reasons: (1) the employee's past record shows that the unsatisfactory conduct will continue; (2) the most stringent form of discipline is needed to protect the system of work rules; or (3) continued employment would inevitably interfere with the successful operation of the business; and

        d. proof by management that just cause exists.

    2. The employee is entitled to *industrial equal protection,* which requires like treatment of like cases.

    3. The employee is entitled to *individualized treatment.* Distinctive facts in the employee's record or regarding the reason for discipline must be given appropriate weight. 1985 *Duke L.J.* 694, 611–612.

After explaining how this theory of just cause would apply, they conclude that:

> The arbitrator's judgment can be guided by a conceptual model of just cause, a model of the sort proposed here. Every decision maker must determine the facts of a case by, for example, resolving questions of credibility. Our model recognizes that the labor arbitrator must do more than that. He must decide whether the employee failed to provide satisfactory work; whether the discipline furthered one of management's legitimate interests; and whether the employer has provided industrial due process; industrial equal protection, and individualized treatment. The value of a systematic model of just cause, in short, lies not in its ability to supply the right answers, but rather in its power to force the arbitrator to confront the right questions. *Id.* at 623.

Daugherty's Seven Tests

The Seven Tests of Just Cause developed by the late Arbitrator Carroll Daugherty have been widely disseminated. Each of the seven tests are reprinted below. This definition of just cause is losing favor among arbitrators and is rarely, if ever, cited by prominent labor arbitrators. In short, the Seven Tests are headed for extinction.

The tests first came under fire by National Academy President John Dunsford, a law professor and arbitrator.[8] This criticism has been restated by two other distinguished arbitrators. Rolf Valtin, also a former Academy President, believes that the great majority of arbitrators do not follow the seven tests in the way Daugherty intended.[9] Arbitrator George Roumell believes each of the seven tests stands alone, and arbitrators will focus in on one key test, as part of their larger analysis of whether the "discipline was reasonable under the circumstances."[10]

Because Carroll Daugherty was the first to propound a definition of just cause, his Seven Tests are noteworthy. They are historically important.

---

[8] Dunsford, *Arbitral Discretion: The Tests of Just Cause,* Proceedings of the 42nd Annual Meeting of the National Academy of Arbitrators (Washington: BNA Books, 1990).

[9] Valtin, *The Just Cause Standard,* 1992 Labor Arbitration Institute (Minneapolis, 1992). Arb. Valtin's critique is lengthy and worth reading. Here, however, is a brief excerpt: [B]ut the Seven Tests purport to provide an all-encompassing umbrella for automatic application in cases. It will not wash. Indeed, it runs counter to what I think is in the first place to be appreciated about the just cause phrase. The beauty of those two little words is that they permit fair resolution of a literally infinite number of contested situations . . . Except as to the obvious principles . . . certainty in just cause cases is an objective which is both misplaced and dangerous. It is misplaced because the field of variables is so vast as to defy definitional efforts except by recourse to endless qualifications. And it is dangerous because there will likely be a loss of fair and realistic results if the variables and their particular contexts are not permitted to play a determinative role.

[10] Roumell, *Just Cause; A Second Look,* Labor Arbitration Institute Detroit Conference, 1993 (Minneapolis: Labor Arbitration Institute, 1993) Arb. Roumell states, "[j]ust cause, i.e., what is reasonable, requires the application of common sense to a given situation. The Seven Tests help pinpoint whether or not common sense has been applied. It may be that in ascertaining whether an employer's actions were reasonable in a given situation, it is not necessary or even practical to apply each of the Seven Tests. It would seem that rather than necessarily apply all Seven Tests to a given circumstance, the circumstances will determine which of the Seven Tests must be met in order to establish just cause.

The Seven Tests of Carroll R. Daugherty

Whirlpool Corp, 58 LA 421 (1972)

Few if any union-management agreements contain a definition of "just cause." Nevertheless, over the years the opinions of arbitrators in innumerable discipline cases have developed a sort of "common law" definition thereof. This definition consists of a set of guide lines or criteria that are to be applied to the facts of any one case, and said criteria are set forth below in the form of seven questions, with accompanying Notes of explanation.

A "no" answer to any one or more of said questions normally signifies that just and proper cause did not exist. In other words, such "no" means that the employer's disciplinary decision contained one or more elements of arbitrary, capricious, unreasonable, or discriminatory action to such an extent that said decision constituted an abuse of managerial discretion warranting the arbitrator to substitute his judgment for that of the employer.

The answers to the Questions in any particular case are to be found in the evidence presented to the arbitrator at the hearing thereon. Frequently, of course, the facts are such that the guide lines cannot be applied with precision. Moreover, occasionally, in some particular case an arbitrator may find one or more "no" answers so weak and the other "yes" answers so strong that he may properly, without any "political" or spineless intent to "split the difference" between the opposing positions of the parties, find that the correct decision is to "chastise" both the company and the disciplined employee by decreasing but not nullifying the degree of discipline imposed by the company—e.g., by reinstating a discharged employee without back pay.

It should be understood that, under the statement of issue as to whether an employer had just cause for discipline in a case of this sort before an arbitrator, it is the employer and not the disciplined employee who is "on trial" before the arbitrator. The arbitrator's hearing is an appeals proceeding designed to learn whether the employer in the first instance had forewarned the employee against the sort of conduct for which discipline was considered; whether the forewarning was reasonable; whether the employer, as a sort of trial court, had conducted, before making his decision, a full and fair inquiry into the employee's alleged "crime;" whether from the inquiry said trial court had obtained substantial evidence of the employee's guilt; whether the employer, in reaching his verdict and in deciding on the degree of discipline to be imposed, had acted in an even-handed, non-discriminatory manner; and whether the degree of discipline imposed by the employer was reasonably related to the seriousness of the proven offense and to the employee's previous record. In short, an arbitrator "tries" the employer to discover whether the latter's own "trial" and treatment of the employee was proper. The arbitrator rarely has the means for conducting, at a time long after the alleged offense was committed, a brand new trial of the employee.

It should be clearly understood also that the criteria set forth below are to be applied to the employer's conduct in making his disciplinary decision *before* same has been processed through the grievance procedure to arbitration. Any question as to whether the employer has properly fulfilled the contractual requirements of said procedure is entirely separate from the question of whether he fulfilled the "common law" requirements of just cause before the discipline was "grieved."

Sometimes, although very rarely, a union-management agreement contains a provision limiting the scope of the arbitrator's inquiry into the question of just cause. For example, one such provision seen by this arbitrator says that "the only question the arbitrator is to determine shall be whether the employee is or is not guilty of the act or acts resulting in his discharge." Under the latter contractual statement an arbitrator might well have to confine his attention to Question No. 5 below—or at most to Questions Nos. 3, 4, and 5. But absent any such restriction in an agreement, a consideration of the evidence on all Seven Questions (and their accompanying Notes) is not only proper but necessary.

The above-mentioned Questions and Notes do not represent an effort to compress all the facts in a discharge case into a "formula." Labor and human relations circumstances vary widely from case to case, and no formula can be developed where the facts can be fed into a "computer" that spews out the inevitably correct answer on a sheet of paper. There is no substitute for sound human judgment. The Questions and Notes do represent an effort to minimize an arbitrator's consideration of irrelevant facts and his possible human tendency to let himself be blown by the variable winds of sentiment on to an uncharted and unchartable sea of "equity."

THE SEVEN QUESTIONS

1. Did the company give to the employee forewarning or foreknowledge of the possible or probable disciplinary consequences of the employee's conduct?

Note 1: Said forewarning or foreknowledge may properly have been given orally by management or in writing through the medium of typed sheets or booklets of shop rules and of penalties for violation thereof.

Note 2: There must have been actual oral or written communication of the rules and penalties to the employee.

Note 3: A finding of lack of such communication does not in all cases require a "no" answer to Question No. 1. This is because certain offenses such as insubordination, coming to work intoxicated, drinking intoxicating beverages on the job, or theft of the property of the company or of fellow employees are so serious that any employee in the industrial society may properly be expected to know already that such conduct is offensive and heavily punishable.

Note 4: Absent any contractual prohibition or restriction, the company has the right unilaterally to promulgate reasonable rules and give reasonable orders, and same need not have been negotiated with the union.

2. Was the company's rule or managerial order reasonably related to (a) the orderly, efficient, and safe operation of the company's business, and (b) the performance that the company might properly expect of the employee?

Note 1: Because considerable thought and judgment have usually been given to the development and promulgation of written company rules, the rules must almost always be held reasonable in terms of the employer's business needs and usually in terms of the employee's performance capacities. But managerial orders, often given on the spur of the moment, may be another matter. They may be reasonable in terms of the company's business needs, at least in the short run, but unreasonable in terms of the employee's capacity to obey. *Example:* A foreman orders an employee to operate a high-speed bandsaw known to be unsafe and dangerous.

Note 2: If an employee believes that a company rule or order is unreasonable, he must nevertheless obey same (in which case he may file a grievance thereover) unless he sincerely feels that to obey the rule or order would seriously and immediately jeopardize his personal safety and/or integrity. Given a firm finding to the latter effect, the employee may properly be said to have had justification for his disobedience.

3. Did the company, before administering discipline to an employee, make an effort to discover whether the employee did in fact violate or disobey a rule or order of management?

Note 1: This Question (and No. 4) constitutes the employee's "day in court" principle. An employee has the right to know with reasonable precision the offense with which he is being charged and to defend his behavior.

Note 2: The company's investigation must normally be made before its disciplinary decision is made. If the company fails to do so, its failure may not normally be excused on the ground that the employee will get his day in court through the grievance procedure after the exaction of discipline. By that time there has usually been too much hardening of positions. In a very real sense the company is obligated to conduct itself like a trial court.

Note 3: There may of course be circumstances under which management must react immediately to the employee's behavior. In such cases the normally proper action is to suspend the employee pending investigation, with the understanding that (a) the final disciplinary decision will be made after the investigation, and (b) if the employee is found innocent after the investigation, he will be restored to his job with full pay for time lost.

4. Was the company's investigation conducted fairly and objectively?

Note 1: At said investigation the management official may be both "prosecutor" and "judge," but he may not also be a witness against the employee.

Note 2: It is essential for some higher, detached management official to assume and conscientiously perform the judicial role, giving the commonly accepted meaning to that term in his attitude and conduct.

Note 3: In some disputes between an employee and a management person there are not witnesses to an incident other than the two immediate participants. In such cases it is particularly important that the management "judge" question the management participant rigorously and thoroughly just as an actual third party would.

Note 4: The company's investigation should include an inquiry into possible justification for the employee's alleged rule violation.

Note 5: At his hearing, the management "judge" should actively search out witnesses and evidence, not just passively take what participants or "volunteer" witnesses tell him.

5. At the investigation did the company "judge" obtain substantial and compelling evidence or proof that the employee was guilty as charged?

Note 1: It is not required that the evidence be fully conclusive or "beyond all reasonable doubt." But the evidence must be truly weighty and substantial and not flimsy or superficial.

Note 2: When the testimony of opposing witnesses at the arbitration appeals hearing is irreconcilably in conflict, an arbitrator seldom has any means for resolving the contradictions. His task is then to determine whether the management "judge" originally had reasonable grounds for believing the evidence presented to him by his own people instead of that given by the accused employee and his witnesses. Such grounds may include a decision as to which side had the weightier reasons for falsification.

6. Has the company applied its rules, orders, and penalties evenhandedly and without discrimination to all employees?

Note 1: A "no" answer to this question requires a finding of discrimination and warrants negation or modification of the discipline imposed.

Note 2: If the company has been lax in enforcing its rules and orders and decides henceforth to apply them rigorously, the company may avoid a finding of discrimination by telling all employees beforehand of its intent to enforce hereafter all rules as written.

Note 3: For an arbitral finding of discrimination against a particular grievant to be justified, he and other employees found guilty of the same offense must have been in reasonably comparable circumstances.

Note 4: The comparability standard considers three main items—the degree of seriousness in the offense, the nature of the employee's employment records, and the kind of offense.

(a) Many industrial offenses, e.g., in-plant drinking and insubordination, are found in varying degree. Thus, taking a single nip of gin from some other employee's bottle inside the plant is not so serious an offense as bringing in the bottle and repeatedly tippling from it in the locker room. Again, making a small, snide remark to and against a foreman is considerably less offensive than cussing him out with foul language, followed by a fist in the face.

(b) Even if two or more employees have been found guilty of identical degrees of a particular offense, the employer may properly impose different degrees of discipline on them, provided their records have been significantly different. The man having a poor record in terms of previous discipline for a given offense may rightly, i.e., without true discrimination, be given a considerably heavier punishment than the man whose record has been relatively unblemished in respect to the same kind of violation.

(c) The words "same kind of violation," just above, have importance. It is difficult to find discrimination between two employees found guilty of totally different sorts (not degrees) of offenses. For example, poor work performance or failure to call in absences have little comparability with insubordination or theft.

7. Was the degree of discipline administered by the company in a particular case reasonably related to (a) the seriousness of the employee's proven offense, and (b) the record of the employee in his service with the company?

Note 1: A trivial proven offense as such does not merit harsh discipline unless the employee has properly been found guilty of the same or other offenses a number of times in the past. (There is no rule as to what number of previous offenses constitutes a "good," and "fair," or a "bad" record. Reasonable judgment thereon must be used.)

Note 2: An employee's record of previous offenses may never be used to discover whether he was guilty of the immediate or latest one. The only proper use of his record is to help determine the severity of discipline once he has properly been found guilty of the immediate offense.

Note 3: Given the same proven offense for two or more employees, their respective records provide the only proper basis for "discriminating" among them in the administration of discipline for said offense. Thus, if employee A's record is significantly better than those of employees B, C, and D, the company may properly give a lighter punishment than it gives the others for the same offense, and this does not constitute true discrimination.

Note 4: Suppose that the record of the arbitration hearing establishes firm "Yes" answers to all the first six questions. Suppose further that the proven offense of the accused employee was a very serious one, such as drunkenness on the job; but the employee's record had been previously unblemished over a long, continuous period of employment with the company. Should the company be held arbitrary and unreasonable if it decided to discharge such an employee? The answer depends of course on all the circumstances. But, as one of the country's oldest arbitration agencies, the National Railroad Adjustment Board, has pointed out repeatedly in innumerable decisions on discharge cases, leniency is the prerogative of the employer rather than of the arbitrator; and the latter is not supposed to substitute his judgment in this area for that of the company unless there is compelling evidence that the company abused its discretion. This is the rule, even though the arbitrator, if he had been the original "trial judge," might have imposed a lesser penalty. In general, the penalty of dismissal for a really serious first offense does not in itself warrant a finding of company unreasonableness.

APPENDIX C

EMPLOYER'S STATEMENT OF THE CASE

(MIDSTATE UNIVERSITY)

MIDSTATE UNIVERSITY'S

STATEMENT OF THE CASE

Contents

STATE OF NITA

COUNTY OF DARROW

DISTRICT COURT

SECOND JUDICIAL DISTRICT

Case No. 0012-05

PAT ROGERS,

        Plaintiff,

v.

MIDSTATE UNIVERSITY,

        Defendant.

MIDSTATE UNIVERSITY'S

STATEMENT OF THE CASE

FACTS

This case involves an appeal of the discharge of an employee by Midstate University. The University discharged Pat Rogers for violating a critical rule of Employment under Article 28 B(1) of the Collective Bargaining Agreement, and specifically Rule 6 of the Rules of Employment and Management of the Off Campus Liquor Store, by selling alcohol to an intoxicated person. The terms of the Collective Bargaining Agreement allow the employee to appeal the discharge and submit the dispute to binding arbitration or to elect to have a judge or jury trial. Pat Rogers has elected to have the matter heard in trial.

In _____ (Month -12), the University received a controversial alumni gift of a liquor store located across the street from the campus. The operation of the Off Campus Liquor Store was highly controversial (*see Metropolitan Daily News* articles), so the president of the University, D. Laterno, developed strict management rules, which included the following provisions: "no alcohol could knowingly be sold to a person who is intoxicated," and "any employee violating these rules could be immediately fired and would lose all University benefits." "Knowingly" is defined as "knowing or should have known the buyer was intoxicated" and "intoxicated" is defined as "anyone over .08 percent blood alcohol." *See* Rule 6: Rules of Employment and Management of the Off Campus Liquor Store. In the advertisement for a liquor store manager, the University explicitly stated its commitment to enforcing restrictions on the misuse of alcohol. *See* Want Ad. Pat Rogers, who applied for the position on **Second Monday, _____(Month -11)**, was offered the position because of Rogers's qualifications and sensitivity to the issues surrounding the liquor store. *See* Letter. Rogers began employment on **First Monday, _____(Month -9)**, and six months later, Rogers passed the probationary period even though Rogers was considered a loner and not a team player. *See* Job Review.

Due to rumors of violations of the campus policy at the Off Campus Liquor Store, Midstate University Chief of Police, M. J. Troy, conducted a stake out of the liquor store on **Friday, _____(Week -6)**. At approximately 8:00 p.m., Troy observed an older man walk unsteadily up the sidewalk on Campus Drive, stagger to the door of the liquor store, and enter the store. The man stood at the counter, approximately three feet from where Rogers was working, and purchased a bottle of single malt, GlenLucy whisky after speaking with Rogers. *See* Initial and Follow-Up Reports. The person then left the store, and Troy immediately approached him. The man, later identified as retired Professor Erik Tolefson, admitted to Troy that he had been drinking that day. He subsequently failed all field sobriety tests given, and his breathalyzer test showed a BAC of .12 percent. *See id.* Troy noticed that Tolefson's eyes were bloodshot and glassy, as admitted by Rogers, and Tolefson smelled strongly of alcohol and urine. *See id.* While Rogers believes that Tolefson did not slur or stagger, Troy observed that Tolefson's clothes were filthy, he uncontrollably swayed while standing, and his speech was very slurred. *See id.* Even though it is Rogers's belief that Tolefson's behaviors were attributable to an illness, Rogers admitted that Tolefson had a tremor in his hand and spoke in a "strange accent." Rogers contends having no knowledge of Tolefson's intoxication; however, this is implausible and lacks credibility because Rogers observed all the signs and signals of intoxication that Troy observed. A reasonable person would have concluded that Tolefson was intoxicated. Rogers's decision to sell whisky to an obviously drunk man was negligent. Rogers should have known Tolefson was drunk and should have at least asked Tolefson if he had been drinking. Troy immediately knew Tolefson was drunk, and a reasonable person would have reached the same conclusion as well.

Rogers was terminated on **Wednesday, _____(Week -5)** for violating the Rules of Employment and Management of the Off Campus Liquor Store. *See* Letter. Rogers has appealed the discharge, and the Union filed a grievance on behalf of Rogers. The two issues at trial are whether Rogers was discharged for just cause, and if not, the extent of damages. It is the University's position that they had just cause to discharge Pat Rogers.

LEGAL ANALYSIS

I.   Pat Rogers's Violation of the University Liquor Store Rule Constitutes Just Cause for Termination.

Article 28, subdivision A(3) of the Collective Bargaining Agreement (CBA) between the University and the State Professional Employee Union, which filed a grievance on Rogers's behalf, states that the University has the right to ". . . demote, suspend, reduce in pay, or discharge employees for just cause." The CBA does not define just cause. It is well settled that when a CBA does not specifically define what constitutes just cause, the issues are left to the arbitrator. *City of Brookville v. Local 2828*, 290 Nita 2d 697 **(Year -26)**. The court has gone on to say that the arbitrator is "free to adopt a reasonable definition of just cause . . . ." *City of Morristown v. Police Officers' Federation of Morristown*, 566 Nita 2d 136 **(Year -9)**. The judge in this case has the same discretion as an arbitrator.

Under Nita Statute, § 43A.33, Subd. 2, **(Year -2)**, relating to state employees, "just cause includes, but is not limited to, consistent failure to perform assigned duties, substandard performance, insubordination, and serious violation of written policies and procedures . . . ." While the courts have not adopted a standard definition of just cause, an arbitrator may use the jury instruction guide as a basis for a definition. *Dilek v. University of Midstate*, 511 Nita 2d 17 **(Year -12)**. The Nita jury instructions state that "a termination is for [just] cause if the employee breached the standards of job performance established and uniformly applied by the employer." *See id.*

The University terminated Rogers for just cause on the basis of a serious violation of the liquor store rules, which clearly state that a violation could result in immediate termination. Furthermore, the CBA does not require a lengthy disciplinary process—instead it states that disciplinary actions are at the discretion of the employer. Also, the discipline imposed should be in furtherance of a legitimate management interest, including the rehabilitation of an employee, deterrence of similar conduct, or protection of the employer's ability to operate the business successfully. *See* R. Abrams and D. Nolan, *Toward a Theory of 'Just Cause' in Employee Discipline Cases*, 1985 DUKE L.J. 594 (June 1985).

The University established strict rules to regulate the management and operation of the liquor store due to the controversy surrounding the University's gift from the Wongs and future operation of the store. The rules included a provision that a violation could result in termination, which emphasized the University's seriousness regarding the operation of the liquor store. It was important for the

University to show the community that the University could responsibly operate the store. In fact, the University explicitly stated its commitment to enforce restrictions on the misuse of alcohol in the advertisement for a liquor store manager. Rogers was well aware of the controversy surrounding the liquor store, the misuse of alcohol on campus, and the strict rules developed by the University to avoid any problems. Rogers knew the standard of employee performance required for this management position before entering into the contract and failed to meet the standard.

II. The Professor Exhibited Such Obvious Signs of Intoxication that Pat Rogers Knew or Should Have Known that the Professor Was Intoxicated.

Under Nita Statute § 340A.592 **(Year -2)**, "no person may sell, give, furnish, or in any way procure for another alcoholic beverages for the use of an obviously intoxicated person." In *Strand v. Village of Waterville*, the Nita Supreme Court provided a helpful interpretation of an "obviously intoxicated person" and stated that "when any person from the use of intoxicating liquors has affected his reason or his faculties, or has rendered himself incoherent of speech, or has caused himself to lose control in any manner to any extent of the actions or motions of his person or body, such person in the contemplation of the law is intoxicated." 245 Nita 2d 99 **(Year -51)**. The court stated that a seller using "usual and reasonable powers of observation" could readily observe an "outward manifestation of intoxication" as described above. *See id.*

In *Moose v. Villages of Mitchell Lake*, the court distinguished the difference between "obviously intoxicated" and "intoxicated." 178 Nita 2d 288 **(Year -36)**. "Obviously intoxicated" was described as being readily and plainly evident, or unmistakable, to the observer. *See id.* "Intoxicated" was described as being "discoverable by reasonable active observation of appearance, breath, speech and actions." *Id.* The difference between the two is essentially that "obviously intoxicated" is a blatant manifestation of signs of intoxication and "intoxication" is evident with use of a reasonable power of observation.

The University's liquor store rules prohibited the sale of alcohol to an intoxicated person. The rules define the standard of care as: the employees "knew or should have known the buyer was intoxicated." The facts indicate the professor exhibited an outward manifestation of intoxication to the degree that Rogers should have known the professor was intoxicated even though Tolefson was only in the store for a short time and with the competing smell of alcohol from a broken liquor bottle. The professor had many obvious signs of intoxication: disheveled appearance, filthy clothing, a wet stain at the crotch of his trousers and the smell of urine, bloodshot eyes, dilated pupils, unsteadiness, slurred speech, body odor, and a very strong smell of alcohol. *See* Police Report. Even without professional training, any reasonable person would be able to detect these signs of intoxication.

III.   Burden of Proof.

The Collective Bargaining Agreement permits the employee to have the matter heard by an arbitrator or to waive the right to arbitration and have a court or jury trial. Pat Rogers has waived arbitration and has elected to have the matter decided at a trial.

In arbitration, the employer, Midstate University, has to prove just cause for the termination. The arbitrator may sustain the termination, reinstate with some suspension, or fully reinstate with or without back pay.

In a trial, the employee, Pat Rogers, has the burden by a preponderance of the evidence to prove there was insufficient cause for termination or any discipline at all. The employee must also prove emotional or physical damage by a preponderance of the evidence.

IV.   Remedies.

Under the Collective Bargaining Agreement Article 28, in an arbitration the employee may be terminated, suspended, or reinstated with or without back pay. Additional damages are not available in an arbitration. Pat Rogers has elected to have the matter decided at trial by a judge or jury, thus the Employee may seek damages in addition to the remedies provided by the Collective Bargaining Agreement. In a trial, the Employee has the burden of proving damages by a preponderance of the evidence.

MIDSTATE UNIVERSITY'S POSITION

Midstate University terminated Pat Rogers for just cause, and the University did not violate its employment contract with Rogers. The standard to be applied for a just cause determination is whether a reasonable person would have known that Erik Tolefson was intoxicated and whether termination was justified under these circumstances. The University's policy regarding alcohol sales at the liquor store was strict and concrete. Rogers knew that selling alcohol to a person who was intoxicated would result in termination of employment. Further, Rogers was well aware of the controversy surrounding the liquor store and assured the University of sensitivity to these issues. The facts support the University's decision to terminate due to Rogers's blatant disregard to the overwhelming number of apparent signs that

Tolefson was intoxicated. *See* Police Report. Based on Rogers's serious violation of the rules and knowledge of the liquor store controversy, Midstate University had just cause to impose the most severe discipline of termination upon Pat Rogers. Since the University has already willingly given Rogers two extra days of pay, Midstate University does not intend to offer anything further. The University does not intend to reinstate Rogers as an employee, offer back pay or interest, give any compensation for future loss of earnings or other damages, and finally, the University does not intend to give Rogers a severance package because employment termination was for a serious violation of the rules.

James Garner
_____

James Garner
Attorney for Employer/Midstate University

APPENDIX D

EMPLOYEE'S STATEMENT OF THE CASE

(ROGERS)

PAT ROGERS'S
STATEMENT OF THE CASE

The two issues at trial are whether Pat Rogers ("Rogers") was terminated for just cause, and if Rogers was not terminated for just cause, the extent of the damages. Both parties have stipulated to the provisions of the Collective Bargaining Agreement ("CBA") between the State Professional Employee Union, which represents Rogers, and Midstate University ("University").

Pat Rogers has elected to have the matter decided by a trial.

FACTS

Rogers was hired to manage the University's liquor store on **Last Thursday, _____(Month -11)**. The University terminated Rogers on **Wednesday, _____(Week -5)**, claiming that Rogers knowingly sold alcohol to an obviously intoxicated person. The University claims that it had just cause to fire Rogers because sale of alcohol to an intoxicated person is a violation of the Rules of Employment and Management of the Off Campus Liquor Store.

University's Position

The University received a contribution in the form of a liquor store. The University's acceptance of this gift has been controversial in the community. The University has also received bad publicity regarding the acceptance of the liquor store gift because of the problems surrounding college students' misuse of alcohol. The University put into practice some very strict rules regarding the operation of the liquor store. *See* Rule 6. In fact, if an employee violated any of the rules, the employee would be fired and lose all employee benefits. The rule at the root of this dispute is that no alcohol could knowingly be sold to a person who was intoxicated. Rule 6 defines "intoxication" as "anyone having a blood alcohol concentration over .08 percent." "Knowingly" is defined as "knowing or should have known the buyer was intoxicated." *Id.*

On **Friday, _____(Week -6)**, Police Chief M. J. Troy ("Troy") conducted a stakeout of the liquor store at the University's request. At 8:00 p.m., Troy observed an older unkempt person, later identified as Erik Tolefson ("Tolefson"), staggering to the liquor store. Once Tolefson left the store, Troy stopped Tolefson and performed some sobriety tests, which Tolefson failed. Troy's report states that under observation, Tolefson was disheveled, unsteady on his feet, used slurred speech, and smelled of alcohol. Tolefson's BAC was a .12 percent. *See* Police Report. Based on this report, the University terminated Rogers. *See* Letter of Termination.

Rogers's Position

The University hired Rogers to manage its liquor store. *See* Letter of Hiring. Rogers did not have any experience running a liquor store; rather, his background consisted of managing coffee shops. Not only did Rogers lack experience in managing and running a liquor store, Rogers did not have much experience with alcohol in general. Rogers was a hard worker and valued the job with the University. The University also valued Rogers. In fact, Rogers's six-month review recommended retention and stated that Rogers was a valuable addition to its team. *See* Rogers's six-month Probationary Review. Rogers was in the process of completing the University alcohol training program, but was forced to miss the class on identifying intoxicated persons due to Rogers's child becoming ill.

Even though Rogers missed the class on identifying intoxicated persons, the University permitted Rogers to manage the store. Rogers is not denying alcohol was sold to Tolefson; however, Rogers did not think Tolefson was intoxicated. Rogers claims that Tolefson looked like a tired old person, who may have been homeless and had a cold. Rogers said that there was no smell of alcohol on Tolefson, nor did he appear intoxicated in any other way. Tolefson was only in the store for about a minute, and Rogers had very minimal interaction with him. It is very important for Rogers to keep this job. Rogers was always very careful not to do anything that would violate employment at the University because it would jeopardize family health insurance, retirement benefits, and the reduced tuition for Rogers's children. Also, Rogers suffered a loss on the sale of the coffee shop business in order to take this job.

ANALYSIS

I. Did the University have "just cause" to fire its employee for allegedly violating a rule of employment?

Because there is a Collective Bargaining Agreement present, the "at will" employment standard is not applicable here. Rather, the Collective Bargaining Agreement trumps all state rules. According to the contract between the University and Rogers, the University cannot terminate Rogers without just cause. However, the University has failed to specially define what constitutes just cause. When a contract term is ambiguous, a court's interpretation must draw upon the essence of the agreement. *State Auditor v. Nita Assoc. of Prof. Employees,* 504 Nita 2d 565 (**Year -13**). Further, when a contract term is ambiguous, it must be construed against the drafter. *Hillig v. Cargon,* 649 Nita 2d 466 (**Year -4**). Here, the drafter is the University; thus, the Collective Bargaining Agreement must be construed against the University.

While Nita law has not defined what constitutes "just cause," it does provide some guidance. One interpretation of just cause is that it means a legal cause that touches the qualifications of the employee and their performance or duties. *See In re County of Carr,* 353 Nita 2d 464 (**Year -22**), citing *Lein v. City of Bloomfield,* 299 Nita 2d 327 (**Year -26**). Thus, the employees' actions must affect their performance. For another example, Nita statutes include the following to define just cause: "consistent failure to perform assigned duties, substandard performance . . . and serious violation of written polices . . . provided the policies and procedures are applied in a uniform, nondiscriminatory manner." Nita Statute § 43A.33, Subd. 2, (**Year -2**).

The University is defining just cause as a violation of its liquor store rules. Pat Rogers has the burden of proof by the preponderance of the evidence that the termination was unlawful because the University did not have just cause to terminate Rogers or for any discipline at all. *See Dilek v. Univ. of Midstate,* 511 Nita 2d 17 (**Year -12**). In *Dilek,* the court held that the University had just cause for terminating a coach because he had distributed sex tapes to his athletes. The court reasoned that such conduct tainted the University's reputation and that the coach failed to fulfill his role as a teacher for young students. Here, selling alcohol to an intoxicated person, especially given the public outrage over the consumption of alcohol, also taints the University's reputation. However, Rogers was hired as a manager to direct the liquor store operation. Further, the real issue comes down to whether Rogers knew or should have known that Tolefson was intoxicated.

II. Can the salesperson knowingly sell alcohol to an intoxicated person when the salesperson perceives the customer to be a tired, old person with a cold?

In Nita, it is illegal to sell alcohol to an "obviously intoxicated person." Nita Statute § 340A.592 (**Year -2**). Additionally, a person selling alcohol has a duty to actively observe the signs of intoxication as a reasonable person would. *Jarvik v. Wortman Municipal Liquor Store,* 227 Nita 2d 898 (**Year -31**). In another case, "for a person to be intoxicated there must be such outward manifestation of intoxication that a person using reasonable powers of observation can see or should see that such person has become intoxicated." *Moose v. Villages of Mitchell Lake,* 178 Nita 2d 288 (**Year -36**).

A. Given Rogers's lack of experience with spotting signs of intoxication, it is reasonable that Rogers believed Tolefson was just a tired, old person with a cold.

M. J. Troy is the Chief of Police for Midstate University. Troy was previously an officer for ten years on the force of the University Police Department. Troy is well experienced in spotting intoxicated people and has a great deal of training in alcohol enforcement. Further, Troy trains people on spotting the signs of intoxication. Troy has also written two articles about alcohol violations that have been published within the last two years. *See* Follow-Up Police Report.

Rogers has very little personal experience with intoxicated people. Rogers was not yet sufficiently trained in identifying intoxicated people before this incident. Rogers missed the last training session, which was to specifically talk about identifying intoxicated people. *Id.* Rogers does not have the background that Troy has to identify someone who is intoxicated.

B. Based on Rogers's background knowledge and lack of training it was reasonable that Rogers saw a tired, old man who had a cold and was possibly homeless.

Rogers, an untrained lay person, acted as a reasonable person would under the circumstances. The fact that Tolefson was unkempt, disheveled, unsteady on his feet, and had bloodshot eyes could reasonably be signs of a tired, old person who had been sleeping rough or had a cold. Further, Rogers did not see Tolefson stumble, stagger, or notice his slurred speech. Rogers did not smell alcohol on Tolefson because the store smelled of alcohol from the broken bottle that had spilled alcohol onto the floor. Rogers was also engaged in a number of tasks.

Troy observed Tolefson as disheveled and unkempt, wearing soiled pants and dirty unlaced shoes. Troy watched Tolefson stagger to the door of the liquor store, pause, and then enter the liquor store without anything in his hands. As Tolefson exited the store, he was carrying a sack containing a bottle of alcohol. Troy then spoke with Tolefson and noticed that Tolefson's speech was slurred, eyes were bloodshot, breath smelled of alcohol, and Tolefson was unsteady on his feet. Troy was focused on Tolefson. Further, it was not until after Tolefson failed the three sobriety tests and blew a .12 on the breathalyzer that Troy *knew* Tolefson was intoxicated.

III. Because Rogers did not knowingly sell alcohol to an intoxicated person, Rogers did not violate the University rules.

Rogers did not knowingly sell alcohol to an intoxicated person, and Rogers did not violate the University rules. To terminate Rogers would be a harsh and inequitable conclusion because Rogers had an excellent employment record with the University and diligently followed all of the rules. This is the only violation made against Rogers.

CONCLUSION

Pat Rogers will prove that by a preponderance of the evidence the termination of Pat Rogers by Midstate University was without just cause and therefore unlawful. Pat Rogers will also prove the damages are significant and include health benefits, three-quarters tuition waivers for Pat Rogers's children, back pay, and future damages for lost wages.

Gena Robins

Gena Robins
Attorney for Pat Rogers

APPENDIX E

MEMO TO SENIOR PARTNER

- PRELIMINARY CASE ANALYSIS -

FOR EMPLOYER (MIDSTATE UNIVERSITY)

TO: Senior Partner

FROM: Associate

RE: Preliminary Analysis of Client: Midstate University

ISSUES

I. Does Midstate's discharge of Pat Rogers violate Rogers's due process rights?

II. Did Rogers knowingly sell liquor to an intoxicated buyer, thus allowing Midstate to terminate Rogers for just cause?

FACTS

One year ago Martin and Julia Wong ("Wongs"), both graduates of Midstate University ("Midstate"), donated the Off Campus Liquor Store ("Store") and its proceeds to Midstate. The Store is located across the street from campus property. The Store has an annual net return of at least $1,000,000.

As a result of the increased use of alcohol by college students, and the controversial nature of the Store, Midstate developed strict rules for the Store, including: no alcohol can be sold to underage persons; no alcohol can knowingly be sold to persons who are intoxicated; and employees violating these rules can be immediately terminated and lose all University benefits.

After Midstate took possession of the Store they advertised for a manager. Pat Rogers ("Rogers"), the owner of a small chain of bagel/coffee shops near campus, answered the ad. Rogers found the benefits of the University system, including reduced tuition for employees' children at the Midstate-run schools and the health and retirement benefits, attractive. Rogers had no prior experience managing a liquor store. Rogers sold the coffee shop businesses and began employment at Midstate nine months ago.

At 8:00 p.m. on **Friday,** _____ **(Week -6)**, Rogers was working alone in the Store. Rogers sold a bottle of liquor to Erik Tolefson ("Tolefson"), a retired Professor of Norwegian studies and philosophy. Rogers claims that Tolefson did not appear intoxicated. However, Midstate University Police Chief, M. J. Troy ("Troy"), watched Tolefson enter the Store and suspected he was drunk. After Tolefson left the Store, Troy observed Tolefson's appearance, smell, stance, and speech. Troy stood further away from Tolefson than Tolefson stood in front of Rogers in the Store and observed Tolefson in a shorter time period and under less favorable circumstances than those inside the Store. The signs and signals demonstrated that Tolefson was intoxicated. Following these observations and as a part of police procedure, Troy also administered a breathalyzer test to Tolefson, which indicated that Tolefson had a blood alcohol content ("BAC") of .12 percent.

After reviewing Troy's report, Midstate terminated Rogers for knowingly selling liquor to an intoxicated person. Through the Union, Rogers grieved the discharge, waived arbitration , and the matter is now set to be decided at trial.

ANALYSIS

I. Rogers could argue discharge violated Rogers's right to procedural due process.

Where a public employee cannot be terminated without just cause, the employment is a protected property interest and entitles the employee to procedural due process protections.

It appears that here at least two of the due process requirements for terminating an employee were not met by Midstate. *See Dilek v. University of Midstate*, 511 Nita 2d 17 **(Year -12)** (listing due process requirements). As a result, Rogers may have an argument that Rogers's due process rights have not been met. However, because the parties have agreed that the issue before the court is whether Rogers was discharged for just cause, the due process argument is unlikely to be raised by Rogers.

II. Midstate has an argument that Rogers knowingly sold alcohol to an intoxicated buyer, and therefore Midstate had just cause to terminate Rogers.

Employees covered by collective bargaining agreements and those employed by federal or state governments generally can be discharged only for "just cause." *Id.* An employer has the burden of proving just cause by clear and convincing evidence. *Dilek*, 511 Nita 2d at 17. Nita courts have not adopted a standard definition of "just cause." *Id.* The jury instruction guide states that "[a] termination is for good cause if the [employee] breached the standards of job performance established and uniformly applied by the [employer]." [*See* Jury Instructions—Appendix I.] This definition of just cause requires that an employer treat employees uniformly when applying job standards. *Dilek*, 511 Nita 2d at 17.

Article 28, A(3) of the Collective Bargaining Agreement between the SPEU, which represents Rogers, and Midstate notes that Midstate may discharge employees for "just cause." Furthermore, one of the Store's rules provides that no alcohol can knowingly be sold to any person who is intoxicated (i.e., BAC over .08 percent). "Knowingly" is defined as "when the seller knows or should know that the buyer is intoxicated." Rogers will contend that while Tolefson looked tired and dirty, he did not stagger or stumble while inside the liquor store. Rogers will also argue that Tolefson did not slur his speech and did not smell of alcohol. Further, Rogers may argue that because Rogers would not have done anything to jeopardize the job or the University, Rogers would not knowingly serve alcohol to an intoxicated person. In addition, Rogers may contend that while Troy may have identified Tolefson as intoxicated, Troy is not an ordinary person because of Troy's extensive training in spotting inebriated persons. Rogers will conclude that because Rogers did not know and had no reason to know that Tolefson was intoxicated, there was no just cause for Rogers's discharge in violation of the contract with Midstate.

Midstate can respond, however, that Rogers absolutely should have known that Tolefson was intoxicated when he made the purchase from Rogers. For instance, Troy indicated that even though Troy observed Tolefson from a greater distance than Rogers and for a shorter amount of time than Rogers, Troy could tell that Tolefson was clearly intoxicated, evidenced by the fact that Tolefson had slurred speech, his breath smelled of alcohol, his eyes were bloodshot, he was unsteady on his feet, and his appearance in general was seriously unkept and unclean. Moreover, Midstate could note that Rogers admitted noticing Tolefson's hand had a tremor in it. Troy should be especially convincing because of experience training officers in alcohol enforcement and the fact that Troy has written two articles about alcohol violations. In addition, Midstate could argue it is Rogers's own fault in lacking the skills necessary to spot an intoxicated individual because of the missed presentation about how to spot intoxicated persons. Finally, no evidence indicates that Midstate would not similarly terminate other employees who violated the liquor store's rules.

CONCLUSIONS / RECOMMENDATIONS

In an arbitration we had a better than 50/50 chance to prove that Midstate University had just cause to terminate Rogers. In the trial, Rogers has the burden to prove unlawful termination. Midstate University's position was reasonable and based on the totality of circumstances. Rogers should have done more than make assumptions. This is not an ordinary case, and because of what was happening at the University surrounding the controversial liquor store operation, we can make a very strong argument that Rogers cannot meet the required burden of proof. Midstate has little to lose in a trial. If we lose, we can work out a settlement and use the verdict as a reason for doing so.

We must show that Rogers's assumptions about Tolefson were wrong and that Rogers should have done more. A good cross-examination of Rogers should demonstrate that Rogers knew the rules and the situation on campus. We can show that Rogers chose not to attend the training and that Rogers saw all of the indications of intoxication. Rogers could have asked Tolefson if he was sick, tired, or homeless, and most importantly, Rogers could have asked Tolefson if he had been drinking. If Rogers had asked, we can assume that Tolefson would have answered the same way he did to Chief Troy: that he had "drank single malt whisky" and had a "snoot full." We can demonstrate that Rogers should not have been careless, given the circumstances, and because of the totality of circumstances in this instance termination is the only just result.

The direct examination of Chief Troy must be carefully structured and detailed to demonstrate that any lay person would know that Tolefson was intoxicated.

Police Chief Troy's testimony and our presentation should be broken into two parts: first, Troy must demonstrate that a lay person would conclude from the facts available to Rogers that Tolefson was intoxicated; second, Troy will be able to give an expert opinion that Tolefson was in fact intoxicated.

As counsel for Midstate, we should enter the trial with the position that none of Rogers's demands should be met. If we must settle, however, Midstate should consider offering the following: extending Rogers's and the family's health insurance coverage until Rogers finds new employment, granting Rogers's children a tuition reduction, and writing a solid letter of recommendation. All of these alternatives will not cost Midstate a significant sum of money. Moreover, Midstate could consider some type of structured settlement deal to cover a portion of lost wages and benefits.

APPENDIX F

MEMO TO SENIOR PARTNER

- PRELIMINARY CASE ANALYSIS -

FOR EMPLOYEE (PAT ROGERS)

TO: Senior Partner

FROM: Associate

RE: Preliminary Case Analysis Client: Pat Rogers

FACTS

A liquor store was donated to Midstate University; however, this contribution caused community controversy. Reacting to this controversy, the University's president developed the Rules of Employment and Management of the Off Campus Liquor Store. One rule was that no alcohol could knowingly be sold to a person who was intoxicated. Any employee violating the rules could be immediately terminated and lose all their employee benefits. A terminated employee could appeal the termination, which would be submitted to binding arbitration. Rogers has chosen, however, to bypass arbitration and proceed to trial on the matter. The remedies at arbitration are limited to reinstatement with or without back pay. Rogers feels, with some justification, that the University will make it difficult for Rogers to work at the University. A trial provides the opportunity for more significant damages, and we have good argument that the University buckled under political pressure and used Rogers as a scapegoat.

Pat Rogers (our client) was hired as the liquor store's manager. On **Friday, _____(Week -6)**, while Pat Rogers ("Rogers") was working alone, Rogers sold a bottle of liquor to retired Professor Erik Tolefson ("Tolefson"). At the same time, Midstate University Police Chief, M. J. Troy ("Troy"), was staking out the liquor store to make sure no rules were broken. Troy, professionally trained to recognize intoxication, approached Tolefson after he left the liquor store. Troy noticed that Tolefson smelled of alcohol, had bloodshot eyes, soiled clothing, slurred speech, and was unsteady, causing Troy to conclude that Tolefson was intoxicated. Troy administered an intoxilyzer test to Tolefson, which determined that Tolefson's blood alcohol concentration (BAC) was .12 percent. Troy confronted Rogers about selling alcohol to Tolefson. Rogers maintained no knowledge of Tolefson's intoxication, but thought that he was a tired, old person who had a cold. Rogers was terminated and has appealed.

ISSUE

1. Was Rogers terminated by the University for just cause?

Discussion

Trial versus Arbitration

The controlling Collective Bargaining Agreement ("CBA") between the University and the State Professional Employee Union ("SPEU"), Rogers's Union, states that "arbitrators shall render determinations of a violation of work rules and the appropriateness of proposed penalties . . . ." CBA, Article 28. Arbitrators are to act within the confines of the agreement; however, if the agreement does not "specifically define what acts constitute just cause for discharge, the parties [leave] this decision to the arbitrator." *Sundquist v. Mid. Teamsters Public and Law Enforcement Employees Union Local No. 320*, 316 Nita 2d 343 **(Year -24).** In this particular case, the alleged just cause is that Rogers "knowingly" sold liquor to an intoxicated person. "Knowingly" is defined as "knowing or should have known the buyer was intoxicated." "Intoxicated" is defined as "a person with blood alcohol content over .08 percent." The decision for the arbitrator, therefore, is to decide whether Rogers's act of selling liquor to Tolefson is just cause for termination. The arbitrator is limited to upholding the discipline, suspending Rogers for a period of time, or reinstating Rogers with or without back pay. Rogers has chosen to bypass arbitration and proceed to trial because the potential damages in a trial are high. If Roger prevails at trial, damages could include past and future wages, health care, and reduced tuition for Rogers's children.

Just Cause

Under the liquor store rules, the University has the burden of proving just cause. According to the jury instructions guide, termination for good cause (being similar to just cause) is found when the employee breaches the job's standard of performance as determined by the employer. *Dilek v. University of Midstate*, 511 Nita 2d 17 **(Year -12)**. In our present case, the University president, D. Laterno, determined that one job standard of performance at the liquor store was that no employee could knowingly sell liquor to an intoxicated person. At face value, it would appear that Rogers obviously breached that standard. First, Tolefson was intoxicated per the definition because he had a blood alcohol content of .12 percent. Second, Rogers should have known that Tolefson was intoxicated because he smelled of alcohol, was soiled from dirt and urine, was unsteady, used slurred speech, and had bloodshot, glassy eyes. While Tolefson was intoxicated, Rogers admits selling liquor to him. This would be a breach of the job standard such that Rogers could be justly terminated.

Rogers, however, maintains that he had no knowledge of Tolefson's intoxication. There are two standards for determining if the liquor seller knew or should have known if someone was intoxicated. One standard involves recognizing a person who is "obviously" intoxicated, and the other involves an affirmative effort to notice intoxication. *Moose v. Villages of Mitchell Lake,* 178 Nita 2d 288 **(Year -36)**. Recognizing obvious intoxication involves "using reasonable powers of observation" to see an "outward manifestation of intoxication." *Strand v. Village of Waterville,* 245 Nita 2d 99 **(Year -51)**. It is not expected that the seller "must subject a buyer to a blood test or urinalysis." *Id.* at 616. Although the BAC can be used as evidence for intoxication, it is not prima facie evidence. *Gustavson v. Edwins,* 419 Nita 2d 331**(Year -18)**. Consequently, although the liquor store's rules defined intoxication as BAC of .08 percent or higher, this is not prima facie evidence that Rogers knowingly sold liquor to an intoxicated person.

Nor did the alcohol smell on Tolefson cause Rogers to consider Tolefson's intoxication. A bottle of Canadian whisky had recently been broken behind the counter, and the whisky smell probably permeated the counter area, masking Tolefson's smell. Finally, Rogers thought that Tolefson was a homeless person who had a cold and an accent—explaining away the "obvious" intoxication signs. Tolefson's intoxication was not obvious to Rogers.

The other standard for knowing if a person is intoxicated requires a "thorough or prolonged observation of the subject's appearance, speech, and action as would in the exercise of reasonable care, reveal to the observer a loss of control of the actions or motions of the subject's person or body in any significant manner . . . ." *Moose* 178 Nita 2d at 288. Under this standard, Rogers should have taken the time to watch, observe, and smell customers to make sure no one buying liquor was intoxicated. Since Rogers was aware of the liquor store controversy and aware of the liquor store rules, perhaps Rogers should be held to this standard. If so, then Rogers should have known that Tolefson was intoxicated; however, Rogers was not trained for this type of observation.

CONCLUSIONS AND RECOMMENDATIONS

Unlike Troy, Rogers was not trained to recognize intoxication. Consequently, Rogers should not be held to the standard of prolonged observation. To Rogers, Tolefson was not "obviously" intoxicated; rather Tolefson was a tired old person with a cold. There is no knowing aspect here, and during trial this fact would need emphasis. Also, although Tolefson had a BAC of .12 percent, this by itself is not prima facie evidence that Rogers should have known that Tolefson was intoxicated.

Through a good cross-examination of Chief Troy, we can demonstrate that Troy is arguably qualified to spot inebriated persons, and he had only one job that evening whereas Rogers had many duties. We can show that Tolefson passed the "walk in the straight line" field sobriety test in the store, and Troy had no idea what Tolefson said or how he acted in the store. Troy chose not to provide the training Rogers missed because of a sick child. Troy should have trained Rogers given the serious nature of the situation. Troy chose not to train and instead chose to try to "catch" someone violating the rules. Rogers did not have Troy's qualifications and did not see everything that Troy saw. What Rogers saw is consistent with Rogers's conclusion about Tolefson.

Since the CBA allows the judge or jury to determine the appropriateness of the remedies, *City of Brookville v. Local 2828 of the American Federation of State, County and Municipal Employees*, 290 Nita 2d 697 **(Year -26)**, while the arbitrator could order reinstatement; we should be able to prove unlawful termination and remedies that include health and benefits, three-quarters tuition waivers for Rogers's children, back pay, future damages for future lost wages.

If we make a strong case at trial, we may be able to negotiate an appropriate settlement before a verdict. The risks of trial are high, but remedies available to Rogers are significantly higher than at an arbitration. The pressure is on the University to resolve this case. We should look for a way to provide the University with reason to settle.

APPENDIX G

SUMMARY OF STATUTES CITED

STATUTES CITED

Nita Statute § 43A.33, Subd. 2, _____(Year -2).

Just cause. Just cause includes, but is not limited to, consistent failure to perform assigned duties, substandard performance, insubordination, and serious violation of written policies and procedures, provided the policies and procedures are applied in a uniform, nondiscriminatory manner.

Nita Statute § 43A.33, Subd. 5, _____(Year -2).

Procedures for discipline and discharge of employees. Procedures for discipline and discharge of employees covered by Collective Bargaining Agreements shall be governed by the Agreements.

Nita Statute § 340A.592, _____(Year -2).

Sales to obviously intoxicated persons. No person may sell, give, furnish, or in any way procure for another alcoholic beverages for the use of an obviously intoxicated person.

APPENDIX H

SUMMARY OF CASES CITED

SUMMARY OF CASES CITED

City of Brookville v. Local 2828 of the American Federation of State, County and Municipal Employees, 290 Nita 2d 697 **(Year -26)**.

City discharged employee for acts alleged to constitute just cause, and the employee's Union filed a grievance, which resulted in the matter being submitted to arbitration. Arbitrator determined that there was no just cause for discharge, but that there was just cause for discipline and fashioned a remedy. The award was appealed and vacated on the ground that the arbitrator had exceeded his authority. The Union appealed, and the Supreme Court held: 1) trial court exceeded the scope of judicial review when it interpreted the collective bargaining agreement in such a way as to place restrictions on the arbitrator that were not found in the agreement or in any written submission of issues; 2) there was nothing in the applicable collective bargaining agreement to preclude the arbitrator from fashioning certain types of remedies; and 3) under all the circumstances, it was within the authority of the arbitrator to find that there was not just cause for discharging the employee, but that there was just cause to impose a lesser discipline.

City of Morristown v. Police Officers' Federation of Morristown, 566 Nita 2d 136 **(Year -9)**.

City brought action seeking review of arbitration award in which arbitrator found that City did not have just cause under terms of collective bargaining agreement to terminate police officer due to his involvement in use of excessive force against arrestee. The District Court affirmed. City appealed. The Court of Appeals held that: 1) City failed to show that arbitrator exceeded his authority under terms of agreement; and 2) City failed to show well-defined, dominant public policy that prohibits police officers found to have used excessive force from being reinstated to police force. Thus, the City did not demonstrate that arbitration award could be vacated on public policy grounds.

Dilek v. University of Midstate, 511 Nita 2d 17 **(Year -12)**.

University coaches petitioned for certiorari to challenge discharges. The Court of Appeals held that: 1) athletic director's failure to follow University's procedural manual by not seeking approval of vice president of academic affairs prior to discharging coaches did not prejudice coaches; and 2) just cause for discharges was proved.

Ferbesher v. Lillian Isenberg Construction Co., 516 Nita 2d 206 **(Year -10)**.

An employee may elect to have a disciplinary matter heard by a judge or jury rather than a labor arbitrator under the terms of a collective bargaining agreement giving the employee that right. Other state law notwithstanding, a collective bargaining agreement may grant employee rights in addition to those provided by state or federal law. A union may elect not to represent an employee in a disciplinary matter when an employee elects to have the matter heard by a judge or jury under the terms of a collective bargaining agreement giving the employee that option to elect to have a matter heard by a judge or jury. The union may choose to retain counsel to represent the employee when the employee elects to have the disciplinary matter heard by a judge or jury, but the union is not required to do so.

Gustavson v. Edwins, 419 Nita 2d 331 **(Year -18)**.

Widow brought action against bar for selling intoxicating beverages to obviously intoxicated person. The District court entered summary judgment for bar owner and appeal was taken. The Court of Appeals held that genuine issue of material fact as to whether patron of bar was obviously intoxicated precluded summary judgment for bar owner in action brought by widow of patron for selling intoxicating beverages to obviously intoxicated person.

Hillig v. Cargon, 649 Nita 2d 466 **(Year -4)**.

Former employee brought action against employer to recover unpaid bonus. The District Court entered judgment on jury verdict for employee. Employer appealed. The Court of Appeals affirmed, and employer appealed. The Supreme Court held that: 1) termination for "good cause" was the same as termination for "cause"; and 2) evidence of employee's competition with employer was inadmissible.

In re County of Carr, 353 Nita 2d 464 **(Year -22)** (citing *Lein v. City of Bloomfield,* 299 Nita 2d 327) **(Year -26)**.

Deputy sheriff discharged for misconduct appealed a decision of an arbitrator denying his grievance and finding he was properly discharged. The District Court confirmed the arbitrator's award and denied deputy sheriff's motion to vacate the award, and the deputy sheriff appealed. The Court of Appeals held that: 1) the "misconduct" standard for discharge of a public employee under the Veterans Preference Act is the same as the "just cause" standard applied by the arbitrator; 2) thus, deputy sheriff was not entitled to a new hearing to determine whether there was misconduct; 3) deputy sheriff's claim for unpaid salary under the Veterans Preference Act was not before the Court of Appeals, where the issue was not raised at arbitration hearing; 4) fact that deputy sheriff had his discharge arbitrated without determining issue of back pay did not bar him from bringing a separate action for recovery of back pay; and 5) factual basis for deputy sheriff's discharge was adequately presented in the arbitrator's award and opinion.

Jarvik v. Wortman Municipal Liquor Store, 227 Nita 2d 898 **(Year -31)**.

In dram shop action, the District Court ordered judgement for defendant, and plaintiffs appealed. The Supreme Court held that it is duty of seller of intoxicating liquor to take such affirmative steps as a reasonably prudent man would regard as adequate to ascertain whether the conduct of a customer manifests such loss of control of actions or motions as would make it illegal to furnish him more liquor; that under the circumstances in the instant case, seller had duty to engage customer in conversation to determine the mater of intoxication; and that instruction that it was not the duty of seller to make specific inquiry to determine the matter of intoxication was fundamental error.

Moose v. Villages of Mitchell Lake, 178 Nita 2d 288 **(Year -36)**.

Action against villages for death of plaintiffs' husband and father in automobile accident allegedly resulting because municipal liquor stores in villages had illegally sold intoxicating liquor to other driver. After entering judgment for defendants based on jury's special verdict finding that although collision was proximately caused by intoxication of other driver, neither village had sold liquor to him when he was obviously intoxicated, the District Court granted plaintiffs' motion to vacate judgment and ordered a new trial, and defendants appealed. The Supreme Court held that granting of instructions that defendants were

Rogers v. Midstate Univ.—Trial

liable if sales were made to other motorists at a time when he was "obviously intoxicated" after statutory amendment had removed "obviously intoxicated" from statute prohibiting sales to intoxicated persons was such fundamental error of law as to justify new trial.

State Auditor v. Midstate Assoc. of Prof. Employees, 504 Nita 2d 565 **(Year -13)**.

Arbitration award reinstating employee of state auditor's office who had been discharged for filing false expense reports was appealed. Award was vacated by the District Court, and the Court of Appeals reversed. On appeal by office of the state auditor, the Supreme Court held that: 1) though employee's conduct would appear to violate well-defined and dominant public policy, it did not follow that award reinstating him on ground that confession indicated intention to reform would violate public policy; and 2) though conduct provided sufficient grounds for arbitrator to find "just cause" for discharge, disagreement with contrary result did not provide sufficient grounds for vacating award.

Strand v. Village of Waterville, 245 Nita 2d 99 **(Year -51)**.

Appeal was taken from order of the District Court affirming actions of city park and recreation board and civil service commission reclassifying park patrolmen as park patrol agents and reducing their salary. The Supreme Court held that city park patrolmen who had been sent notice of proposed reclassification of their position to park patrol agents and who had been orally briefed on implications thereof, including reduction in salary, but who failed to file protest as provided by civil service rule at time changes were made effective in _____**(Year -34)** and did not file formal objection until January _____**(Year -32)**, waived whatever rights they had at date of their reassignment.

Sundquist v. Mid. Teamsters Public and Law Enforcement Employees Union Local No. 320, 316 Nita 2d 343 **(Year -24)**.

State sought to vacate arbitration award in favor of its employee and his Union. The District Court vacated award on ground that arbitrator had exceeded authority given him by parties, and employee and Union appealed. The Supreme Court held that arbitrator did not exceed his power by commenting on severity of penalty and noting that it would be overturned notwithhstanding that stipulated issue was limited to whether employer had "just cause" to discipline employee.

R. Abrams and D. Nolan, *Toward a Theory of 'Just Cause' in Employee Discipline Cases*, 1985 Duke L.J. 594 (June 1985).

CONCLUSION—"When the parties to a collective bargaining agreement adopt the standard of just cause, they expect that an arbitrator will apply the principle in the manner they intend. Unfortunately, the parties rarely explain their intentions in any detail. By examining the interests of the parties in a discipline case, an arbitrator can make sound judgments about the probable expectations of the parties. The common adherence of labor and management to general principles of fairness, efficiency, rehabilitation, and deterrence, indicates that both wish the disciplinary system to accomplish similar objectives."

Appendix I

Jury Instructions

(Just Cause)

PART I
PRELIMINARY JURY INSTRUCTION
(Given prior to the evidence.)

The following jury instructions state general principles that may apply to this case and that may be used at the discretion of the trial judge.

A. Introduction

You have been selected as jurors and have taken an oath to well and truly try this case. This trial will last one day.

During the process of the trial there will be periods of time when the court recesses. During those periods of time you must not talk about this case among yourselves or with anyone else.

During the trial, do not talk to any of the parties, their lawyers, or any of the witnesses.

If any attempt is made by anyone to talk to you concerning the matters here under consideration, you should report the fact to the court immediately.

You should keep an open mind. You should not form or express an opinion during the trial and should reach no conclusion in this case until you have heard all of the evidence, the arguments of counsel, and the final instructions as to the law that will be given to you by the court.

B. Conduct of the Trial

First, the attorneys will have an opportunity to make opening statements. These statements are not evidence and should be considered only as a preview of what the attorneys expect the evidence will be.

Following the opening statements, witnesses will be called to testify. They will be placed under oath and questioned by the attorneys. Documents and other tangible exhibits may also be received as evidence. If an exhibit is given to you to examine, you should examine it carefully, individually, and without any comment.

It is the right of counsel to object when testimony or other evidence is offered that the attorney believes is not admissible.

When the court sustains an objection to a question, the jurors must disregard the questions, and the answer if one has been given, and draw no inference from the questions or answer or speculate as to what the witness would have said if permitted to answer. Evidence stricken form the record must likewise be disregarded.

When the court sustains an objection to any evidence, the jurors must not give such evidence any more weight than if the objection has not been made.

When the evidence is completed, the attorneys will make final statements. These final statements are not evidence, but are given to assist you in evaluating the evidence. The attorneys are also permitted to argue, to attempt to persuade you to a particular verdict. You may accept or reject those arguments as you see fit.

Finally, just before you retire to consider your verdict, you will receive further instructions on the law that applies to this case.

PART II
FINAL JURY INSTRUCTIONS
(Given at conclusion of evidence.)

A. Introduction

Members of the jury, the evidence and arguments in this case have been completed, and you will now receive instructions concerning the law.

The law applicable in this case is stated in these instructions, and it is your duty to follow those instructions. The order in which the instructions are given is not significant. You must not single out certain instructions and disregard others.

It is your duty to determine the facts, and to determine them only from the evidence in this case. You are to apply the law to the facts and in this way decide the case. You must not be governed or influenced by sympathy or prejudice for or against any party in this case. Your verdict must be based on evidence and not on speculation, guess, or conjecture.

From time to time it has been the duty of the court to rule on the admissibility of evidence. You must not concern yourself with the reasons for these rulings. You should disregard questions and exhibits that were withdrawn or to which objections were sustained.

You should also disregard testimony and exhibits that the court has refused or stricken.

The evidence that you should consider consists only of the testimony of the witnesses and the exhibits that court has received.

Any evidence that was received for a limited purpose should not be considered by you for any other purposes.

You should consider all the evidence in light of your own observations and experiences in life.

Neither these instructions nor any ruling or remark indicate any opinion as to the facts or as to what your verdict should be.

B. Opening Statement/Closing Arguments

Opening statements are made by the attorneys to acquaint you with the facts they expect to prove. Closing arguments are made by the attorneys to discuss the facts and circumstances in the case and should be confined to the evidence and to reasonable inferences to be drawn therefrom. Neither opening statements nor closing arguments are evidence, and any statement or argument made by the attorneys that are not based on the evidence should be disregarded.

C. Credibility of Witnesses

You are the sole judge of the credibility of the witnesses and of the weight to be given the testimony of each. In determining what credit is to be given any witness, you may take into account the witness's ability and opportunity to observe; manner and appearance while testifying; interest, bias, or prejudice; the reasonableness of the witness's testimony considered in the light of all evidence; and any other factors that bear on the believability and weight of the witness's testimony.

D. Expert Witnesses (when applicable)

You have heard evidence in this case from witnesses who have testified as experts. The law allows experts to express opinion on subjects involving their special knowledge, training and skill, experience or research; but while their opinions are allowed to be given, it is entirely within the province of the jury to determine what weight shall be given their testimony. Jurors are not bound by the testimony of experts; their testimony is to be weighed as that of any other witness.

E. Direct and Circumstantial Evidence

The law recognizes two kinds of evidence—direct and circumstantial. Direct evidence proves a fact directly; that is, the evidence by itself, if true, establishes the fact. Circumstantial evidence is the proof of facts or circumstances that give rise to a reasonable inference of other facts; that is, circumstantial evidence proves a fact indirectly in that it follows from other facts or circumstances according to common experience and observations in life. An eye witness is a common example of direct evidence, while human footprints are circumstantial evidence that a person was present.

The law makes no distinction between direct and circumstantial evidence as to degree of proof required, and each should be considered according to whatever weight or value it may have. All of the evidence should be considered and evaluated by you in arriving at your verdict.

PART III

PROPOSED AND OPTIONAL JURY INSTRUCTIONS

A. Claims and Defenses

The court will now instruct you on the claims and defenses of each party and the law governing the case. You must arrive at your verdict by unanimous vote, applying the law, as you are now instructed, to the facts as you find them to be.

The plaintiff is Pat Rogers. The defendant is Midstate University.

Both parties agree on the following:

- The Off Campus Liquor store associated with Midstate University ran an ad for a store manager.

- Pat Rogers applied for the job and was hired.

- Pat Rogers owned a business before becoming employed with Midstate University.

- Pat Rogers's six-month job review recommended continued employment.

- Plaintiff's employment compensation package included an annual salary of $55,000, full health and dental coverage for Plaintiff and Plaintiff's legal dependants, and a vested retirement after a six-month probationary period. These benefits are worth 33&1/3 percent of employee's salary. Additional benefits include three-quarters tuition waiver for children's elementary school attendance (full tuition is $5,000 annually), three-quarters tuition waiver for children's high school education (full tuition is $10,000 annually), and three-quarters tuition waiver for qualified enrollment at Midstate University (full tuition is $20,000 annually).

- Pat Rogers sold liquor to Professor Erik Tolefson.

- Midstate University terminated Pat Rogers.

Plaintiff Claims

- On _____ (Wednesday, Week -5), Plaintiff was wrongfully terminated.

- Defendant's conduct was in violation of the termination procedures of the Collective Bargaining Agreement and Rogers's terms of employment for the following reasons:

  a. Plaintiff did not violate the terms of the Collective Bargaining Agreement or the terms of employment.

  b. Plaintiff did not intentionally and knowingly sell alcohol to an intoxicated person.

Defendant Denies

- Midstate University denies it wrongfully terminated Rogers without just cause.

- Midstate University denies Rogers suffered damages as a result of Defendant's conduct in terminating Rogers.

B. Just Cause

Termination is for just cause if the employee breached the reasonable standards of job performance established and fairly and uniformly applied by the employer.

Just cause includes, but is not limited to, consistent failure to perform assigned duties, substandard performance, insubordination, or serious violation of written policies and procedures.

C. Damages

The term "damages" means a sum of money that will fairly compensate a person injured. Damages may be recovered for past and future harm. However, it must be proved such future harm is reasonably certain to occur.

A party seeking damages must prove the nature, extent, duration, and consequences of harm.

In determining the amount of damages to the plaintiff, you are to consider the following:

1. The value of lost earning and the possible loss of future earnings. If future earning capacity has been destroyed or reduced by termination, you may determine the present case value of such loss or reduction of future earning capacity considering the age, health, skill, training, experience, and industry of the party.

2. The value of lost benefits, including medical and dental insurance costs; educational tuition waivers for the Plaintiff's children, from their elementary to post-secondary educations; and pension and retirement benefits.

D. Burden of Proof

In order for the Plaintiff to prevail in any claim, the greater weight of the evidence must support such a claim. Greater weight of the evidence means that all of the evidence by whomever produced must lead you to believe it is more likely that the claim is true than not true. If the evidence does not lead you to believe it is more likely that the claim is true than not true, then the claim has not been proved by the greater weight of the evidence.

The greater weight of the evidence does not necessarily mean the greater number of witnesses or the greater volume of testimony. Any believable evidence may be a sufficient basis to prove a fact.

E. Concluding Instruction

The court did not in any way and does not by these instructions give or intimate any opinions as to what has or has not been proven in this case or as to what are or are not the facts of the case.

No one of these instructions states all of the law applicable, but all of them must be taken, read, and considered together as they are connected with and related to each other as a whole.

You must not be concerned with the wisdom of any rule of law. Regardless of any opinions you may have as to what the law ought to be, it would be a violation of your sworn duty to base a verdict on any other view of the law than that given in the instructions of the court.

STATE OF NITA   **DISTRICT COURT**

COUNTY OF DARROW   **SECOND JUDICIAL DISTRICT**

PAT ROGERS,

      Plaintiff,

   v.   **SPECIAL VERDICT**

MIDSTATE UNIVERSITY,

      Defendant.

We, the Jury, in the above-entitled matter, make the following findings of fact:

Question 1   Did the Plaintiff prove by a preponderance of evidence that Defendant did not have just cause to terminate Plaintiff?

      Yes _____   No _____

Question 2   Did the Plaintiff suffer economic damages as a direct result of the termination?

      Yes _____   No _____

Question 3   Did the Plaintiff suffer loss of benefits including: medical and dental insurance costs, educational tuition waivers for Plaintiff's children from their elementary through post-secondary educations, pension and retirement benefits?

      Yes _____   No _____

Regardless of your answers to Questions 1, 2, and 3, you must answer Question 4.

Question 4   What sum of money will fairly and adequately compensate Plaintiff for all damages resulting from the termination?

      Wages and Earning Capacity $ _____

      Benefits:

      • Medical and Dental Insurance Costs $ _____

      • Education Tuition $ _____

EXHIBITS LIST

[Exhibits Located on CD]

Exhibit 1: **Collective Bargaining Agreement—Article 28**

(Witnesses: Pat Rogers, Police Chief Troy and President D. Laterno)

Exhibit 2: **Metropolitan News [University Sells Soul for Alcohol Money]**

(Witnesses: Pat Rogers and President D. Laterno)

Exhibit 3: **Metropolitan News [Opponents of Liquor Store Gift: Shame on 'U'!]**

(Witnesses: Pat Rogers, Police Chief Troy, and President D. Laterno)

Exhibit 4: **Metropolitan News [Manager Wanted—Want Ad]**

(Witnesses: Pat Rogers, Police Chief Troy, and President D. Laterno)

Exhibit 5: **Rogers's Application Letter**

(Witnesses: Pat Rogers and President D. Laterno)

Exhibit 6: **Rogers's Resume**

(Witnesses: Pat Rogers and President D. Laterno)

Exhibit 7: **Letter of Hiring from Alex Margolis**

(Witnesses: Pat Rogers and President D. Laterno)

Exhibit 8: **Rules of Employment and Management of the Off Campus Liquor Store**

(Witnesses: Pat Rogers, Police Chief Troy, and President D. Laterno)

Exhibit 9: **Six-Month Probationary Period Job Review for Pat Rogers**

(Witnesses: Pat Rogers, Police Chief Troy and President D. Laterno)

Exhibit 10: **Incident Report of Chief of Police, M. J. Troy**

(Witnesses: Police Chief Troy and President D. Laterno)

Exhibit 11: **Photograph of Tolefson's Receipt of Purchase from Off Campus Liquor Store**

(Witness: Police Chief Troy)

Exhibit 12: **Photograph of Tolefson's Bottle of GlenLucy in Bag**

(Witness: Police Chief Troy)

Exhibit 13: **Photograph of Tolefson's Bottle of GlenLucy in Bag**

(Witness: Police Chief Troy)

Exhibit 14: **Photograph of Tolefson's Bottle of GlenLucy**

(Witness: Police Chief Troy)

Exhibit 15: **Letter from Pat Rogers to President D. Laterno**

(Witnesses: Pat Rogers and President D. Laterno)

Exhibit 16: **Termination Letter from President D. Laterno to Pat Rogers**

(Witnesses: Pat Rogers, Police Chief Troy, and President D. Laterno)

Exhibit 17: **Metropolitan News [Liquor Store Manager Fired for Selling Booze]**

(Witnesses: Pat Rogers, Police Chief Troy, and President D. Laterno)

Exhibit 18: **SPEU Grievance Form**

(Witnesses: Pat Rogers, Police Chief Troy, and President D. Laterno)

Exhibit 19: **Letter from Pat Rogers to President D. Laterno**

(Witnesses: Pat Rogers and President D. Laterno)

Exhibit 20: **Letter from President D. Laterno to Pat Rogers**

(Witnesses: Pat Rogers and President D. Laterno)

Exhibit 21: **Follow-Up Report by Chief M. J. Troy**

(Witnesses: Police Chief Troy and President D. Laterno)

Exhibit 22: **Follow-Up Incident Diagram Prepared by Police Chief, M. J. Troy**

(Witnesses: Pat Rogers, Police Chief Troy, and President D. Laterno)

Exhibit 23: **Letter from Pat Rogers to Union Advocate**

(Witnesses: Pat Rogers and President D. Laterno)

Exhibit 24: **Letter from President D. Laterno to Attorneys Representing Midstate University**

(Witnesses: Pat Rogers and President D. Laterno)

Exhibit 25: **Letter from Rogers to Laterno re Electing a Trial**

(Witnesses: Pat Rogers and President D. Laterno)